THE CAPTAINS

BOOKS BY JACK CLARY

THE CAPTAINS   (1978)

THE GAMESMAKERS   (1976)

THIRTY YEARS OF GREAT FOOTBALL   (1975)

THE WASHINGTON REDSKINS   (1974)

THE CLEVELAND BROWNS   (1973)

JACK CLARY

THE CAPTAINS

New York   1978   ATHENEUM

LIBRARY OF CONGRESS CATALOGING IN PUBLICATION DATA
Clary, Jack T.
   The captains.
     1. Athletes—Biography. 2. Leadership.
3. Group games. I. Title.
GV697.A1C6 1978   796′.092′2 [B]   77-15830
ISBN 0-689-10871-0

PUBLISHED SIMULTANEOUSLY IN CANADA BY
MCCLELLAND AND STEWART LTD.
MANUFACTURED BY AMERICAN BOOK—STRATFORD PRESS,
SADDLE BROOK, NEW JERSEY
DESIGNED BY KATHLEEN CAREY
FIRST EDITION

TO MY MOM

for direction, faith and love

INTRODUCTION

It is still every athlete's dream to be captain of the team. With younger people, the honor is often a measure of popularity or skill, or, ideally, one's ability to lead and still succeed as a skillful player in every game. With older athletes in college and professional sports, being captain is the result of a great deal of thought given by team members to the type of person they want to lead them.

Regardless, the position means that one person (or two or three, in the case of co-captains or tri-captains) above everyone else on the team is considered someone special. Size or physical skills often are overshadowed in favor of how a person acts or is capable of handling difficult situations. It is almost impossible to define what makes a person that way, yet you recognize it when it happens—you experience a sense of confidence and trust in an individual who, regardless of how difficult something may be, will find a way to overcome the problem and help you succeed.

We have seen in some old movies how the team captain was always the most handsome player, the fastest runner, the shiftiest halfback, the most intelligent student . . . and the guy who always seemed to have the prettiest girlfriend. That make-believe captain was all fun and fancy, the product of someone's imagination, made to be the perfect human being and a model for everyone to copy.

Ah, but there really are no perfect human models for us to copy. Some are better than others, and what makes them better is the kind of person they are. This has nothing to do with great athletic skills, a handsome face, or getting the highest marks. It would be nice if every one of us had all of these attributes, or even if every team captain had them. But that will never happen. Yet it is not impossible for every person and every captain to be a good person, one who thinks of others before thinking of himself or herself.

That really is a team captain's main responsibility. All the honors and recognition which go with the job don't mean a thing if a captain neglects this. It is great to be seen walking to the middle of the field to call the coin toss or to lead the team out of the dressing room before a game, or to carry the winning trophy home from the awards dinner. But those things are superficial if the captain can't honestly say he or she has given every ounce of energy to help the team.

That is why the easy part of the job is being selected; the hard part is doing all that is expected of you. Good captains take their jobs seriously, and instead of becoming one of the gang try to be their own person, making decisions on what they feel is correct, not on what everyone may want to do. Often that is difficult because it means going against the popular outlook. But if a captain truly believes he is correct, then he must stand for that belief. In short, a captain must be courageous and absolutely positive that before asking someone else to follow an example, he or she is doing the very best possible job.

Even the captains in those old Hollywood movies tried to tell us that. They always seemed to be trying to help someone who was having difficulty mastering classroom work; or who had unwittingly become involved with some villainous men; or who had lost his best girlfriend. Nothing seemed to matter to those make-believe captains until every problem was solved and their team had won the big game—which it invariably did, even with the captain or the person he helped coming to the rescue in the final seconds and snaking his way through hordes of tacklers to score the winning touchdown.

The men in this book are superb examples of what those imaginative Hollywood scriptwriters had in mind, but even these men fall short of being perfect, as do all of us. They may miss a block or throw an interception; or run to the wrong base or make an error; or miss a crucial foul or make a bad pass; or get caught up the ice or fail to forecheck or backcheck. They may not always have been the fastest, quickest, or most successful players on their teams, nor were they the most brilliant in school or always the ones who had the prettiest girlfriends.

But the one thing each man has is the reason they were selected as team captains: they had the faith and trust of their teammates and never failed to live up to that faith and trust.

Points, batting averages, touchdowns, goals—none of that, they all say, really means much if your teammates don't trust you or have faith in what you do. And, they add, it is not necessary to be the team captain to achieve this faith and trust. In fact, each of these men acknowledges that every person can be his or her own captain by doing what is right. It is that simple.

Every man in this book says the captain's job really is not to be the main man but to be the one who harnesses the energies of every teammate and gets them working toward the common good of everyone; the person who, if there is a problem, will sit and listen to a teammate and try to help; and who believes strongly enough in the team and teammates that he or she will stand with them through every difficulty.

The captains I knew long before I sat down to write this book had tremendous pride in that job, and years after they stopped playing still have the same feeling. Rarely—from the time I was in high school through college and being involved with athletes for many years

—have I not found a team captain who took his job seriously and tried to live up to all that was expected of him and all that he expected of himself.

The lessons I have learned from these fine men I have known and from the nine captains who are featured in this book are the ones I hope you will discover and be able to apply to your own lives. They are the athletes who deserve your attention and who should serve as models to you, in and out of sports. They are the ones who truly are successful in the one area that counts the most—they are good persons.

Jack Clary
Stow, Massachusetts

CONTENTS

THE CAPTAINS

PHOTOGRAPH BY FOCUS ON SPORTS

PETE ROSE

"Pete Rose creates the atmosphere around here."

Sparky Anderson, manager of the Cincinnati Reds, couldn't have put Pete Rose's role as team captain more succinctly. He echoed the impressions of every member of his team and those held by almost every player who ever competed against the Reds during Pete's long major league career.

What Sparky Anderson said about Rose is precisely what you'd hope any coach or manager would say about his team captain. It is what being captain is all about. Though every captain approaches his job according to his own personality, Pete has created a style that seems to fit all the situations and personalities he encounters when he plays.

Pete is the ultimate in a professional athlete. He is totally dedicated to his job and it is not exaggerating to say that he cannot wait to get to the ballpark each day and to spring training each year. An off day in the schedule annoys him, and even though he is past the mid-thirties, he refuses to take an occasional day off. His entire life revolves around the game of baseball as played by the Cincinnati Reds. He talks about it to his teammates and if they are busy, he'll go across the field to the opposing dugout and talk about it with the opposition. And if they're busy too, he'll go down the foul lines and talk to the groundskeepers.

You get the distinct impression watching Pete Rose playing third base—and before that, left field and second base—that he is a man totally happy with his job. It is easy to see nothing appeals to him more than baseball. There he is with his sleeves rolled up, exposing massive forearms resembling driveshafts of giant locomotives; his pants are rolled just below his knees so that his sturdy legs can be free to churn their way on the basepaths, or to pursue ground balls or pop-ups; his hamlike hands crunch up his glove before every play so that it almost disappears. Look at all of that and you see a man ready for work.

Pete Rose is a craftsman in the same way that a blacksmith or a shoemaker or a steelworker is. There is nothing fancy about what these people do. Certainly there is nothing fancy about Pete Rose sliding head first into a base, or twitching his bat impatiently as he waits for each pitch, or hustling around the basepaths, legs pumping, hat flying off, a look of steely-eyed determination etched on his face.

All of that is the key to Pete's successful job as team captain. He goes out each day and tries to set an example for every player to follow. He knows that every player will not do precisely what he does and he doesn't expect that will ever happen. But he knows it is a rare day when he doesn't give a total effort. That's what he hopes every player will follow, in his own way, through his own style.

It is easy to see why as a boy Rose admired an outfielder named Enos Slaughter. Slaughter played most of his big league career for the St. Louis Cardinals and his most famous play occurred in the seventh game of the 1946 World Series against the Boston Red Sox. With the score tied, he raced all the way home from first base on a single to left field. Normally, players will never try to score from first base on a single to left field, particularly one that did not roll too far, because the relay to home plate is the shortest from any spot in the outfield.

But shortstop Johnny Pesky of the Red Sox hesitated for just a split second in handling the relay, and Slaughter never broke stride as he rounded third base and pounded across home plate with a cloud-of-dust slide to give the Cardinals the winning run and the world championship. That play has always been called one of the game's most daring, but then Enos Slaughter was always called one of the game's most daring and exciting players. So is Pete Rose.

5

The first rule in Rose's book of being a good captain is leadership by example. He doesn't limit this just to playing in a game but applies it to the way he practices each day and his mental approach to baseball, even to putting on his uniform or sitting with his teammates in the clubhouse. His involvement in a game is total. He keeps a mental book on every opponent. He knows what opposing pitchers will throw to him in every situation, what outfielders can throw strongly from each area of the field, which players can run well, which will not take an extra base if there is a slight opportunity they will be thrown out . . . in short, he is in the game from start to finish and he tries to keep his teammates equally alert mentally.

"I think the main thing I do for my teammates is getting them to concentrate on developing good habits," he says. "It's awful hard for some guys who want to play every day and can't. I've always felt that if a guy didn't want to play every day, then you don't want him on your team. But as long as he is there, he should have the desire to be the best he can every minute. Most of us have a tendency to work only on that which we can do well and do the other just good enough to get through. Not me. I've had to work too hard to accomplish everything I've done. If I can do it, then so can anyone else."

However, Rose makes the distinction that the way he plays baseball has nothing to do with his being the Reds' captain. In other words, he doesn't go out each day and play as hard as he can just to have the other players follow his lead.

"The only way I know how to play is to go at every game with as much intensity as I can muster," he says. "I play to win, not to motivate people. Sure, if giving a guy a pat on the back or saying a few words of encouragement will help a team, I'll do that. Where I think I really help is to try and take an extra base if I can, or stand up to anyone who tries to muscle us. I've never backed down to anyone, in any situation.

"Most players don't have to play with my style because I think most players in the big leagues, who are regulars, have more talent than I. I've heard it said that I can't run or I'm not a great fielder. But no one ever has said I can't hit. Maybe I can't run fast but I know when to run. Maybe I can't catch but I know when to throw. That's doing the job every day."

All of that is contagious to the other Cincinnati players. They have so much respect for his energy and talent that they do not take offense when he comes up and says something about their play. For one thing, Pete does not try to upstage his manager and all of his comments are directed at getting more out of each player rather than creating a total mood within the clubhouse.

"When I was a rookie," shortstop Dave Concepcion remembers, "Pete made it a point to talk with me. It wasn't anything private or important. He wanted to let me know that he knew what it was like for a rookie and that if things ever went bad, he would help me all he could. Sometimes during a game, we may drag a little and Pete will say, 'Davey, let's get that ball around the infield a little faster and see if we can pep things up.' Or he'll remind me, 'Be aggressive at the plate. Don't lay back. Go after that pitcher.' And if I get a hit, he'll say, 'Great, that's the way. Now go three-for-three or four-for-four. Don't let up.' "

That is one form of leadership—the enthusiasm one player can generate in another. There is a certain electricity and excitement about Rose whenever he steps on a field. You know it is as natural for him to be there as in his own home. He always seems in command of every situation, creating other situations as he goes. All are positive, all seem to involve the actions of his teammates, regardless of who they are or their status.

Joe Morgan, whose locker is next to Pete's in the Cincinnati clubhouse, is a totally different kind of person and player. But he responds to Rose's actions with great respect. Morgan is one of the Reds' best players and his positive reaction to Pete as a leader by example has a rippling effect throughout the team. It is another form of the "core leadership" that other captains have referred to as being so important to overall team success.

"I'll come into the clubhouse some days and I tell myself there is no way I'm going to play today," Morgan says. "Then Pete comes in. It's just another day for him, even though we might not have gotten home until the early morning hours because of a late night game. He'll sit next to me and begin to talk about that game or about who is supposed to pitch against us that day. Before long, he's got me wanting to play. In fact, I feel so good after talking to him I can hardly believe me.

8

"I know," Morgan adds, "he isn't talking to me just to get me in the lineup. He's that way naturally, with all of his enthusiasm and his drive. But you can't be around him too long before it rubs off on you. I've always thought that even if Pete wasn't the captain, he'd be that way. It's the only way I've ever known him.

"When I played for Houston, Pete had been in the big leagues for a few years. But he'd come over and talk to me before a game and he'd encourage me. 'You're going to be a star in this league pretty soon,' he'd tell me. That meant a lot coming from a player with his reputation. He didn't have to do it because I wasn't a teammate. But that is the way he approaches everything in baseball. He's got such a positive outlook that it really gets to you."

Sparky Anderson remembers when Don Gullett first came to the Reds as a rookie. Later to be one of the team's best pitchers during their 1975 and 1976 world championship seasons, he was like any other rookie in the big leagues—a bit confused and awestruck.

"Pete would get Don and take him to dinner," Sparky remembers. "They'd talk baseball game situations and probably anything else Pete had on his mind. All of that served to make Don feel at home with the team and to steady him down. It's been that way ever since I became the team's manager. Pete—and this is his idea—would get with the young players and make them feel a part of our organization. It probably is the chief reason why we've been very successful in bringing young players in and seeing them develop so quickly. It's an atmosphere that he creates for everyone."

Anderson is the first to admit that having a player of Rose's great drive and ability is the best thing that could happen to a major league manager. He knows—and they've talked about it—that Pete never would try and usurp his authority. Anderson and everyone else on the Reds know that Pete is not a yes man but have enough respect to allow Anderson to handle his job as he should.

Sometimes he'll come to his manager before a team meeting and say, "Why don't you chew me out. Maybe it will wake everybody up a bit." And sometimes that's exactly what happens, whether or not Pete deserves it (Anderson says rarely has that ever been the case). But the impact of seeing one of the team's highest paid and most productive players being strongly criticized has its effect.

"Everyone thinks that Pete is hustling and doing his job, but when he gets chewed out, that brings them up short," Anderson says. " 'Boy if he chews out Pete, I'd better watch it,' they tell themselves. And the whole tempo seems to pick up immediately."

Anderson has a certain glow when he talks about Rose. He should, because Rose has helped make his tenure as manager one of the most successful in Cincinnati history—four National League pennants and two world championships in the first eight seasons on the job. Anderson admits Rose wouldn't be any different if another man managed the Reds. That is because no one involved with Pete every day will ever change his approach and the stability he brings to the ballpark. That makes it easier for all concerned to understand him.

"There is a great ease and comfort working with Pete," Anderson adds. "In all the years I've been with him he hasn't changed. He might not agree with a lot of the things I say but he'll do them. That's leadership. I know there have been times when he's been mad at me but I never have felt uneasy around him. Those things pass but he stays the same."

Both men have a strong relationship with each other. Anderson knows that often younger players are reluctant to take their problems to the manager, yet they must have some outlet. On the Reds, it is Rose. Pete listens to them and then talks with Anderson about the situation. With older players who have problems or complaints, it is the same way. Pete does not make any decisions but both the players and the manager know that he can be trusted to see that the situations are worked out to everyone's satisfaction.

"The key word is stability," Anderson says. "Our captain is the one player who has been the most successful over the longest period of time. He's proven he's popular. Why, when I became manager, he came to me and said, 'I make the most money. Anything you want done, you tell me and I'll get it done.' And he always did. Every day he goes out on the field and sets a good example for every player on the team. You can't ask any more from a captain. In fact, having a captain who didn't play that way could be a disadvantage. The moment he began to let up or take the short cuts, everyone else would follow his example. We never have to worry about that in Cincinnati as long as Pete is the Reds' captain."

Rose indeed is rare among professional athletes in his role as captain. While some teams may have factions where the captain is on one side and another group of players is on the other, Rose has everyone's respect.

"Just watching Pete play gave me goose bumps," says former Reds player Daryl Chaney, who added: "In fact, I got goose bumps just listening to him talk.

"I remember during a heat wave in Cincinnati, we were sitting around complaining about playing when it was so hot. 'I hope it's 110 degrees out there,' Pete told us, 'because I know I'll be strong and the pitcher will be weak.' What can you say when someone has that attitude? I know I figured that if he can play when it's 110 degrees, then so can I."

Often Rose will assure his teammates with his spirited play. Anderson says he can't recall how many times, after a pitcher has gotten Pete out, that he'll trot to the dugout via the pitching mound and always have something to say.

"He'll yell at the guy, 'You ain't got nothin'. I'll get you the next time.' He'll yell it right to his face. Sometimes these pitchers really get mad and they'll buzz Pete the next time he comes up. That only makes him more determined to get a hit and I think he does more often than not."

Determination certainly is a strong point in Rose's leadership makeup. Morgan said he anguished for his friend during the 1976 season when Pete had a chance for the National League batting title and then hit a five-game slump in which he didn't get a hit.

"If he had only taken a day off, he could have licked it," Morgan says. "He was just dead physically during this time but he wouldn't sit down. I think throughout the latter part of his career he could have accomplished more if he had taken a day off here and there. But that's not his style and I respect him for it."

If anything, Morgan says, Pete goes out and works harder when he is in a slump, "just hits and hits and hits until he starts hitting in a game. And if there is anyone on the team in a slump, he figures they should do the same thing. He'll go out after a game and pitch batting practice for anyone who says he needs extra hitting. That's his way of helping. He doesn't often give advice about technical points unless asked but he'll do everything else to help."

Rose has had to overcome more than an occasional batting slump during his big league career. He jumped from what then was the Class A Sally League to a starting job with the Reds in 1963. In so doing, he took the regular second baseman's job from Don Blasingame, a popular veteran who ironically had his best major league season the year before. Many of the Red veterans, friends of Blasingame's, resented this peppery newcomer and quite often he found himself alone. That was when Pete made up his mind that he would never allow the same thing to happen to any rookie player.

Nor has Pete Rose, through the years, been the most popular visiting player in places like New York's Shea Stadium or Dodger Stadium in Los Angeles. Sadly, some fans in those parks have thrown things at him during a game. When he played the outfield, there were games when the Reds took him off the field until the fans stopped throwing.

Nor were there always happy times with opposing players. Much of the resentment in Shea Stadium came from a scuffle he had in 1973 with New York Mets shortstop Bud Harrelson when the two got tangled up during a double play situation at second base. Unfortunately, the fans took up Harrelson's cause by throwing things at Pete.

Rose never backed down. As happens anytime he's challenged his response was even stronger, almost directed as much toward the fans as it was toward the Mets. There were some ugly words written and shouted, and some potentially dangerous crowd confrontations.

"More than anything I ever did, the Mets thing gained me the respect of players all over the league," he says. "Certainly, it was that way on the Reds. We were flying home from New York after that series and Chief Bender, who is in charge of the team's scouting department, said to me, 'You know, I've been watching you play ever since you came to the big leagues and I never knew what kind of player you were until this series. I really respect the way you play the other teams.' "

However, Rose never will agree that what he did brought his team any closer.

"We lost the game," he says with characteristic frankness, which also tells something about the perspective he places on team success and his own personal dilemmas. It reflects also the perspective in which he places his own role as team captain. While pointing to his role as a leader by example, he cites other factors.

"First," he says, "a captain must be liked by all of his teammates. Secondly, he must be respected. Next, he has to be friendly. He can't show favoritism toward some players and exclude others. He must get along with everyone and of course, he must play hard to set an example. I'd never follow anyone who was dogging it or giving in to little aches and pains that kept him out of the lineup.

"It's easy to tell someone, 'Do as I say.' But I'll never ask anyone or tell anyone to do anything that I wouldn't do myself. I'm a 'Do as I've already done or do as I do' leader. You can always read a book on the right way to play but if I tell a guy that he could have taken an extra base on a ball hit to left field, he knows that I would have done it. In that case, he should try and do it too."

This is not a rule, or even a means of leading, that applies to every sport. In baseball, every man in the lineup takes his turn at bat and fields his position. In football, there are different responsibilities for different positions. A defensive end cannot tell a quarterback how to throw the football or when it should be thrown, just as the quarterback cannot tell a defensive end how he should rush a passer or play a certain kind of run.

That is where the players on each team recognize talent and have respect for their leader. Pete takes care, if his team loses, to stifle any comments until the next day

15

or when a situation is a bit more favorable. He knows that he can talk to almost any member of his team and get through to him. He certainly will not talk about the more elementary facets of the game with stars such as Morgan, Johnny Bench, or George Foster, though Foster will listen to anything Pete has to say to him at any time he may wish to say it.

"The approach is very important," Pete says. "I know when I can get through to Joe Morgan. He and I don't agree with each other all the time but we respect whatever differences we have. With Joe or anybody else, you try and make them see that the point you are trying to make is correct. I remember telling Dave Concepcion that when he hits the ball good, he should take off for first base thinking about making the hit a double, not going to first base and then seeing what develops. I've often thought if he did that, if many of our players did that, we'd get a lot more doubles.

"Baseball is a game of challenge. The pitcher challenges the hitter and vice versa. And when you get a hit, you've got to challenge that fielder to be perfect in how he fields the ball and how he throws it. To be successful, you've got to know your opponents, which ones play aggressively, which ones can't throw."

There was a game in 1977 against the Pirates in Cincinnati when Pete Rose looped a ball into right field. A ball hit like that generally will spin to the right and into the corner once it bounces on Riverfront Stadium's artificial turf. Rose knew this and thought about a double all the way. But the ball hit, popped up into the air and into the right fielder's glove. Yet that wasn't the end of the play. Rose still challenged the Pirate outfielder and got thrown out at second base. It took a perfect throw but Rose didn't mind. He complimented the outfielder for his physical and mental strength.

"He knew what I was going to do," Pete declared. "He answered the challenge because he was ready if he ever got the ball in position to throw me out. There are some outfielders who just pick up the ball and throw it without any real plan. On a play like that, if anyone had thrown the ball to first base, thinking I had just made a wide turn, I'd easily have reached second base. Anything other than a perfect throw to second and I would have been safe."

Rose puts a great deal of emphasis on being mentally prepared and also avoiding physical errors. He says he'd rather strike out four times than make an error and his long list of Golden Glove awards for fielding excellence at second and third base, and in the outfield, are proof of his ability. He takes ground balls by the dozen to improve his fielding and cut down on physical errors, and works on the mental part "by staying in the game."

"I make it a point on every play to tell the left fielder and shortstop how many outs there are and what possibilities we may have to make a play. If there is a power hitter at bat and our pitcher has a 2–0 count, I'll look over and see who's in the on-deck circle. If it's a punch-and-judy hitter and there are two outs, I'll tell the pitcher, 'Don't fool with this guy. Don't give him anything good to hit. There's an easy one ready to come up.' All I'm doing is making him cognizant of what is happening."

Again, Pete takes that upon himself as a team leader. He says quite frankly he doesn't expect anyone else to do it because he doesn't think there is another player who is as attentive as he is. It's not unusual for him, between pitches, to check the crowd for old friends, carry on a conversation with the opposing third base coach and be ready as soon as his pitcher releases the ball, knowing instantly what he will do should it be hit toward him. No one can recall the last time he threw to a wrong base or made a truly serious mental blunder.

It is why he can urge his teammates to be aggressive in their play and then get across his message. By experience, he knows that there are big league ball players who do not pay attention during a game. They do not, in their minds, have the possible situations plotted out—how many out, how many on base, where will the throw be, where will it come from—situations which determine every play.

"If I'm going to bat, I know exactly what I'm going to do," he says. "For example, suppose the other third baseman has just been called out on strikes with men on base to end an inning. I know he's upset about that and his mind probably is on that last pitch more than it is on what I might do. So that is the time I may lay down a bunt. I've always felt, and I've told it to other players, that if you play against a person with equal talent and you play for that extra edge, you'll always come out on top."

Pete lives in fear of someday not running out a ball and then watching the first baseman bobble it badly enough that he could have been safe. He remembers vividly a game where Cincinnati trailed St. Louis 8–0, with two out in the seventh inning. He hit an easy grounder back to the pitcher. Just as he always did, Pete ran as hard and as fast as he could to first base. What happened? The pitcher made a lazy throw and Pete beat it for a hit. Before the Reds were finished, they scored eight runs and tied the score. Lou Brock's home run in the ninth inning won that game for St. Louis. But for anyone who ever asked about running out every ground ball, Pete Rose made his point.

Much of this great awareness and determination stems from his father's influence. His dad was involved for years as a player in all major sports around the Cincinnati area, so Pete was exposed from the first day he could walk. He remembers his father telling his first Little League coach that if Pete always would be allowed to switch-hit regardless of the situation, he would guarantee that his son would be available for every game. This meant giving up family summer trips, but his father stuck to his bargain and Rose now is baseball's all-time switch-hitter.

When he was playing in the minor leagues, Pete would receive letters from his father reminding him to work hard and always to hustle. Even after he was a regular on the Reds, his dad would wait for him after a game if he felt Pete had not hustled throughout the entire nine innings.

"You don't look like you're hustling," he would say to his grown son, who even by that time had won a couple of National League batting titles. "Is there something wrong with you? You don't look like you're playing with the intensity I know that you have."

Now it is Pete Rose who does that with his own teammates. It is all a part of being captain of the Cincinnati Reds, and part of being Pete Rose. There probably isn't a better combination in all of major league baseball.

BOB JOHNSON

Bob Johnson knows what it's like to be a team captain. He has been one at every level of football competition, beginning in Midget League back in his home town of Cleveland, Tennessee, through junior and senior high school, and during his senior year at the University of Tennessee where he was an all-American center. When the Cincinnati Bengals began playing in the National Football League in 1968, who was their offensive captain? Bob Johnson.

There have been others who have been captains at every level of competition, but what makes Johnson so unique is that he became an NFL captain in his rookie season. In professional football, a man generally is elected or selected to be a captain after he has proven himself both as a leader and as a player. He need not, as is sometimes the case in high school, be the best player but he certainly must be one who is consistent in his play and dedicated to his job.

Bob Johnson circumvented those rules. Coach Paul Brown thought so much of his ability that he made him the first player drafted by Cincinnati. In selecting him to be his team captain, Brown bypassed other players with more age and experience, in some cases with more talent.

Other players' talent or experience meant nothing to Paul Brown, a man who must be considered the greatest professional football coach in the game's history. He knew what he wanted in a captain because some of the sport's supreme players had been on his Cleveland Brown teams where leadership on and off the field was considered a prime ingredient in the team's success.

Paul's greatest players were not always his team captains but those whom he selected always had the qualities which made them great people. These were men like Lou Saban, Mike McCormack, Walt Michaels, later to become successful coaches themselves. They adhered to a set of principles—"the eternal verities of truth, honesty, and discipline," Paul Brown calls them—that were the building blocks upon which he built his other great teams at Washington High School in Massillon, Ohio, his national collegiate champions at Ohio State, and his great service teams at Great Lakes Naval Training Center during World War II.

So before he ever selected Bob Johnson to play for the

Bengals, Paul Brown took pains to find out as much about Johnson's leadership ability as he did his playing ability. Brown has never regretted the decision.

"We selected Bob as our first draft choice," Brown said years later, "because he represented the kind of player who also was an exceptional young man. He had leadership qualities that were most unusual. In a word, he was a class person and a class football player. He had strength, speed, intelligence and never failed to utilize those qualities while playing for the Bengals."

These are words of praise which Paul Brown has reserved for very few of the thousands of players he has coached. Therefore they must mean something.

If you get to know Bob Johnson and what he stands for, you can easily see what his former coach means. While many players with the awards Johnson has won since his high school days might have an inflated impression of themselves, Johnson puts himself into a very clear perspective. Remember, he was not only an all-American football player in college but also graduated with honors; he has played in pro all-star games and is a vice president of U.S. Shoe Company in Cincinnati when not playing football. Success, then, is no stranger to him.

"I have used whatever ability God has given me and tried to do the best I could in everything in which I was involved," he says quite simply. "That's the way I was brought up to play football and to approach my life's work."

That is something we've all heard before, probably the

most basic formula used by any successful person. But what makes Johnson a bit different in its application is that he has not limited himself only to helping himself. He has accepted leadership roles, positions that might allow him to help others, and then tried to carry out those roles to their fullest extent. He's never worried about whether it meant he was the most popular guy, or the most talented, or the wealthiest. When he became a team captain on every level of competition, he took the job for what it meant at that time, and did the best he could to be successful with it.

This was something he learned from Harold Henslee, his high school coach back in Cleveland, Tennessee. Johnson remembers him as being tough but very firm and very fair with every player. He demanded that each boy hustle all the time and would stand for nothing but a total effort, in every practice and every game. The lessons he learned on his high school playing field were the cornerstones that helped build his success at Tennessee and with the Cincinnati Bengals.

"I think if you get started like that, you never settle for anything less," he says now. "I can be disappointed if I come off the Bengals' practice field and feel that I didn't work well. There were times when I had to sit out a practice because of an injury and I felt guilty about it. I don't think that's particularly unhealthy. I think it's good. There are people who might say I had some sort of hang-up for feeling that way but I've always felt that you owe it to the people who employ you to do your job every day."

That is one reason why Paul Brown named him the Bengal offensive captain without Johnson ever having played a league game. The Bengals in those days were an assortment of very young players like Bob and older, experienced players who had come in an allocation draft that was supposed to give the team a supply of proven talent. Some of those older players had ten years' experience, some had been all-pro in the old American Football League, others were washed up or no longer wanted by their original teams for a variety of reasons.

"Some of those players were better than I was but that didn't seem to faze Paul Brown," Bob says. "There was less leadership by talking and more lead-by-example under his direction. What could I have told a six- or eight-year veteran? But I didn't have to say too much and the older players accepted me as a captain on that basis. With the conglomeration of people we had, no one player could have told them too much. But keeping the enthusiasm going was something else because the important thing was to make it happen on the practice field. We were so far behind the other teams that we tried to improve a bit each day in practice. The role of any captain in that situation is to set a good example. The coaches will do the talking and the teaching but it's up to the players to maintain the enthusiasm and to keep things moving."

This was how he began, as he says, "to grow into the job" as captain of the Bengals. First, he had to grow as a player, but unlike captains of most other professional teams, who do that without other responsibilities, he also had to grow into the role of being a team leader. That meant getting to know every player, not always on a buddy-buddy basis but to be accessible enough so that he always could communicate with them on any matter they felt worthwhile.

He readily admits any growing pains were eased by the atmosphere created by Paul Brown. Never did coach Brown tolerate troublemakers, malcontents, or malingerers, so the potential for trouble was never great. It was, Bob says, "A great place to grow as a player and to exercise the leadership expected of a team captain."

However, in Bob's mind, leadership on a team is not an individual responsibility. He cites "a core leadership" on the Bengals that has been very successful in helping that team compile records never achieved by any so-called "expansion" sports franchise. For example, Cincinnati was in the NFL playoffs in the third year of its existence and then twice more within the first ten seasons. There were teams in the NFL that never even had a winning record in their first ten seasons, so the influence of Bob and some of his fellow players who made up the "core leadership" must have had some effect.

"You must remember," he says, "that in the tight little world of football, where there are forty people on a team, idle words can be pretty meaningless. There must be leadership by example. Not only by me as a captain but by others on the team who either are in leadership positions, such as a quarterback, or who are recognized stars.

28

"I remember when Archie Griffin joined the Bengals. He came from Ohio State where he was the only player ever to win the Heisman Trophy two consecutive years and had been an all-American running back for three years. There were a lot of guys on the Bengals ready for him to be a smart aleck. But he fooled them, and impressed me. He had only words of encouragement for other players during the practice and he worked harder than anyone during his rookie season.

"Do you know what happened? He wound up earning everyone's respect by the positive things that he did and said. He didn't give anyone a chance to pin a label on him or to knock him. From that point on, he became part of the core leadership on the Bengals because he had earned respect by his own efforts. I always thought that it was a super way for a player, who had his background and his success, to begin a professional career.

"But that doesn't have to be unique only to a player of Archie Griffin's magnitude. The biggest part of being a leader is that when you want to lead, be sure you are doing something worth following. In football, it means knowing your assignments and not making any mistakes, and being in good shape so that you can play or practice with total effort. If you find a player blowing assignments or going only at half speed because he's not in shape and then trying to either encourage or correct his teammates, you'll soon find that no one is paying any attention to him.

"I'm not saying that a player won't make a mistake in

a game or won't get beaten on a play. But when that happens it's important that his teammates know that there's nothing lacking in his overall effort or approach to the game."

That is particularly true for the player who is team captain. For Johnson, it always meant a little extra pressure to make sure, as he puts it, "that my own house is clean and in order, before I go criticizing someone else's."

Being a captain helped Bob Johnson to grow as a person. It placed added pressure on him to practice and play as well as he could. Yet he recognizes that in recent times it has been the tendency of some to look down and make fun of a person who is in a leadership position, particularly someone who may be considered an "honorary" leader such as a team captain. He knows too, from his own years in junior and senior high schools, that many young people are sensitive to the taunts and jibes of others when they assume these positions of leadership. Often a young player will give in to the natural inclination to "join the gang" and slough off his job. Experiences like those happen to professional players too.

"The secret," he says, "is the way you approach the job of being captain, or being a leader. If you are overbearing, always berating people to 'do it my way,' or if you just preach about hustle on the practice field but do nothing yourself, then you'll fail. But if you follow Archie Griffin's example and come in, work hard, and let people see you giving everything you can, then you will be a successful captain, or leader."

30

Johnson has always been very careful to keep separate those areas where he can be captain from those where he really should not tread. That's the easy part. Where it becomes tricky is in between, as in situations where he might use his position to try and influence a fellow player's actions. There are some, including Bill Johnson, his coach at Cincinnati after Paul Brown retired, who feel that such areas are a coach's responsibility. As the coach, Bill Johnson had the overall responsibility for the team's welfare and Bob Johnson, his captain, was under his jurisdiction. Yet both men were able to clearly define the responsibilities each felt in his job so there never was any conflict.

"Anything that happens regarding the morale of the squad or the physical fitness of the squad is in my domain as head coach," Bill Johnson maintains. "I always want to know of such problems and confront them myself. A team is a very delicate mechanism because there are so many different personalities involved. To be successful, a coach must achieve as delicate a balance of all those personalities as he can and then try and maintain that balance.

"I always believed that, on such a basis, a team deserved more consideration and thought than does one man. If you tell your captain, 'There's a problem with so-and-so. Go straighten him out,' what you'll soon have is a pro-captain faction and an anti-captain faction. I always wanted it to be pro-coach or anti-coach because that is where the responsibilities lay."

Bob Johnson agrees with this thinking. He never went

31

to another player and told him flat out, "Shape up!" If matters ever reached that stage, it was the head coach's responsibility to do something about it because the situation probably had become serious.

Yet there are times when he as captain and the other team leaders have gone to a player who isn't performing well and headed off such serious confrontations. Sometimes after players move into a large city they allow their personal lives to interfere with football. Often, these are younger players who for the first time have a regular income and some notoriety, and they lose some of the perspective of what they should be doing.

"I think it's important to say to them, 'You've got to realize how important that playing football is to you right now. You've got a chance to play for six, eight, or ten years and really start your life with a tremendous edge on people your own age.' You do it because there are forty other players who are looking to the sport as a means of livelihood, to get the same good start in life the younger player should be thinking about. A football team is like an assembly line. If one guy slows it down, nobody does as well as they should.

"Of course, all of this depends on the player himself and how I would approach him as the captain of the Bengals. I have made it a rule in such situations never to be overbearing, regardless of the situation. Sometimes that can be tough because emotions play a part. But if I come on and begin demanding or ordering, then the guy will just click me off."

In professional sports, particularly, a captain must be careful how hard he pushes his thoughts on somebody else. That somebody else often is the head of a family, who is tending to his own career and you don't often tell a guy how to run his career. If you do, it is done with great care and always in a positive manner.

"I can't subscribe," Bob Johnson says, "to a very popular philosophy of today, namely: 'Everyone should be allowed to do his own thing.' Football teams really don't work that way. When our quarterback gets sacked, one man isn't to blame. Often there are four or five. We all depend on each other. That's why the one area where you can be the least bit demanding is when it involves lack of effort. There's no excuse in pro football for that. Often young players don't realize this is only a five-month deal and a lot is concentrated into such a short period of time. That means not jeopardizing how well you play. Our workday is very short, nine-thirty in the morning until about four in the afternoon. The mental aspects are not overbearing, so there never is an excuse for not being prepared and for blowing an assignment.

"In the heat of a game you'll miss an assignment now and then because of confusion. But when you know a guy flat out isn't paying attention or refuses to really buckle down mentally, then I think this presents a good case for the captain and the team's core leadership to put pressure on him to work harder at his job."

Bob remembers some of his Cincinnati teammates who made up this type of core leadership. Jim LeClair, a linebacker good enough to play in the Pro Bowl, was one who practiced with almost the same intensity with which he played. Sometimes he'd get involved in some extra pushing and shoving with his teammates during practice, including Bob Johnson. That stirred everyone up a bit. No one let down yet no one got to the point of being violent. But every player could sense LeClair's intensity and their only response was to try and be as intense.

Ken Anderson, the Bengal all-pro quarterback, was another who was as thorough as possible. A quarterback is the acknowledged leader of a team on the field and it is necessary that he live up to that responsibility if the rest of the team is to follow. Kenny did, at all times. It rubbed off on players like Rufus Mayes, an all-pro tackle who was a perfectionist about anything he did on a football field.

"Rufus was an absolute nut about getting his drills correct," Johnson remembers. "That may sound silly after a player has done it for fifty straight practices. But to want to do it right every single day is a sign of leadership. We once had another player named Howard Fest, who was an offensive guard. He'd stay out after practices sometimes and drill on running across the field to block a defensive back. I used to stay with him and I would work at it just as long and hard as he did, even though I was in better shape than he was."

Johnson admits the quickest way to get a young player's attention and to get him thinking about the team concept of the game is to see the team leaders working harder than all the rest. Young players, regardless of

34

their status in college, are still in awe of the older professionals when they join a team. Among the first things they check are the established players and what they are like.

"We're aware of this every year," Johnson says. "We always seem to find ourselves hustling at practice, almost being careful to set a good example. That carries some weight in the eyes of the younger players and it strengthens our own leadership. They don't dare try to lag behind because they know they'll have to fight many obstacles to make the team. Not keeping up is the kiss of death."

Johnson can draw marked differences between his job as the Bengal team captain and what he was called upon to do in high school and college. In high school, there was a core leadership idea that revolved around the four or five best players on the team. They were the stars, the ones who would go to college and everyone looked up to them. That's why Bob Johnson took his job seriously as captain of the Cleveland, Tennessee, team, just as he took it seriously when elected captain of Tennessee's Volunteers before the 1967 season.

"At Tennessee, the team captains were responsible for curfews," he remembers. "Going around and telling people it's time to go to bed, particularly if the people are twenty-one or twenty-two years old, can be a bit touchy. It's even touchy in professional football at training camp when the assistant coaches come around and tell grown men who have families that they have to go to bed at a certain time.

"But when a player does it to other players it can be a

real test of exactly how strong you are as a captain. I never remember ever having any serious problems and I accepted the responsibility because it was my job."

Johnson also remembers his Tennessee coach, Doug Dickey, as one who placed a great deal of responsibility for leadership on his captain. In Bob's senior year, Dickey instituted a program calling for every player having to run a mile within six minutes on the first day of fall practice. Johnson didn't think he could do it and went to his coach to let him know.

"You're the captain, Bob. You have to do it," Dickey replied. "If you don't do it, how can I ask anyone else to do it?"

"He was absolutely correct," Johnson adds. "Coach Dickey even talked me into staying at school that summer to take some extra courses. Of course, while I was at summer school he also saw to it that I got myself into good enough condition so that I would be ready for that six-minute mile run. I ran it, maybe just barely, but I finished within the six minutes. So did every player on that team who was a part of our core leadership."

At the end of Bob's senior season, Tennessee was invited to play for the third consecutive year in a post-season bowl, this time in the Orange Bowl against Oklahoma. Bob's team had beaten Tulsa in the Bluebonnet Bowl when he was a sophomore and defeated Syracuse in the Gator Bowl when he was a junior, but when this invitation came the players were not enthusiastic about going.

It surprises many to discover that not every college football team, or player, really wants to play in a bowl game every year. Bob and many of his teammates had not been home for Christmas since their freshman season and the luster of the bowl game had dimmed. As often happens any time an invited team is reluctant to attend, the school and athletic department try to exert pressure on them to accept the invitation. It means a great deal of extra revenue, national television exposure, as well as a chance to show off the football program to interested high school prospects.

"Some of my teammates were pretty adamant about not wanting to go," he remembers. "They looked on it as nothing more than another month's practice to play one more game. Our coaching staff agreed there would be extra work but liked to point out that we'd be on national television and playing in the Orange Bowl would be something we'd remember the rest of our lives.

"As captain, the players came to me and expressed their opinions. It meant a little negotiating with the coaches to try and satisfy everyone. But before I ever got to the coaches there was the matter of trying to sort out all of the points the players were trying to make and put their case in such a way that we could bargain.

"Actually," he adds, "the whole thing was kind of funny because it all boiled down to what kind of curfew we would have. The coaches wanted ten-thirty, we wanted midnight. We compromised and both sides gave up forty-five minutes, agreeing to eleven-fifteen. But I agreed with my teammates at the time that there should have been some concessions. After all, we were doing all the work and the school was getting all the glory and revenue. I feel now that players with no eligibility remaining should be paid for playing in post-season games. Everyone thinks a reward for going unbeaten or 10–1 is a bowl game but it's not always that much fun for the players."

Such decisions never arise in professional football. Post-season play is what every player strives to attain because it means not only more money but a chance to say that he and his team are the best. Players on winning Super Bowl teams prize the championship rings they get more than the $18,000 per man payoff. It is a symbol to everyone that the player is a champion.

"You get to wear those rings," says Paul Brown, "because your team has players like Bob Johnson. There are many teams with plenty of talent who never get to the Super Bowl or any championship game because they do not have class people like him. I mean people who are good football players and good people.

"We knew what we were getting with Bob. After we drafted him we knew we didn't make a mistake even before he came to training camp because he went off to play for the College All-Stars and was elected their captain, also. This came from fifty of college football's best players, from every section of the country, every conceivable background and system, who had been with him only a few weeks. That is something special."

Bob remembers the day Paul Brown appointed him captain.

"Coach Brown called in Frank Buncom and me. Frank had played several seasons with Kansas City and had been an all-pro player. I was still having my problems learning how to play in the pros. In fact, I never really considered professional football as a career until I was drafted in the first round. I was getting my degree in engineering and figured I'd graduate and go to work for some company. But coach Brown changed all that and when he told me I was to be his offensive captain, it shook me a little. But he was very reassuring and told Frank and me that he had given it much thought through the pre-season and that he felt both of us could perform the leadership roles he felt were so important if this team was to succeed."

Much of what Paul Brown looked for in his captain really counts on the field during a game. To be successful a team must maintain its consistency for all sixty minutes. It is here that Johnson sees his role and that of the team's core leadership as being vitally important.

"It doesn't matter whether we're playing the worst team in the league in a pre-season game or playing in the Super Bowl, there has to be a total effort by every player," he says emphatically. "There have been times in a game when we've been playing sloppily and I'll call the huddle and say, 'Okay, we've got to get going. This is ridiculous. We're not playing the way we should and we're going to look back on this and regret it.'

"Those words aren't limited to me. There are times when anyone who sees this situation should speak up and get everyone's attention. That's individual leadership and it is vital when things don't go well in a game.

"On the other hand," he adds, "we could be playing the Steelers and losing 10–0 early in the second quarter. Then it is time to step in and say, 'Okay, let's not panic. We've got plenty of time. Everyone just do your own job and we'll come out of this fine. Win your own battles and don't worry about other people.' "

Sometimes in the heat of a game when things aren't going too well, players will complain to one another. "You've got to make this block," one might say. Or, "Why didn't you throw the ball? . . . Why didn't you catch the ball? . . ." Again, Johnson says the captain or one of the team's leaders should step in and say, "Okay, forget about that. We can talk about it tomorrow. Let's play the next play." Football is a game of each player depending on the other, and there must be enough leadership on the field to be sure that the game doesn't break down into a series of individual conflicts.

"The worst thing that can happen to a lineman," Bob says, "is to blow his pass blocking and then see the defensive man sack his quarterback. That offensive lineman has to wipe that from his mind immediately and get ready for the next play. On the field, the emotions of every player whiz by because everything happens so fast. You can't stand out there and dwell on something. Of course, your words of encouragement might not make that lineman feel any better but you've got to say something to try and make sure he'll concentrate on the next play and be successful."

Since football is an emotional game, Johnson takes great care to see that personal emotions don't trample personal feelings. Gone are the days when a quarterback such as Bobby Layne, a fiery leader for the Detroit Lions and Pittsburgh Steelers several years ago, would yell at one of his linemen who missed a block.

"I don't want a quarterback yelling at me, 'Block that guy,' " Johnson says very candidly, "because as soon as he throws a bad pass I'm going to yell at him and say, 'Throw the ball.' But if you have an experienced man trying to tell a younger guy how to do something, that's okay. What is harmful is when you've got one guy screaming at another guy for physically missing an assignment or dropping a ball or blowing a tackle. That doesn't do any good. The player is a professional earning his living and he knows if he's fouled things up."

There also are other areas during a game when a captain must make decisions. One is in penalty situations where he must decide, sometimes with guidance from his bench, what options to exercise. That isn't confined only to accepting or declining them but also to knowing the rules well enough to be sure that his team is getting a fair shake.

One of the first great lessons he learned in this regard occurred in a game against the Cleveland Browns after he had been playing three or four years. One of the

Bengal running backs fumbled a lateral, and defensive tackle Jerry Sherk of Cleveland scooped up the ball and ran for about eight yards until he was tackled. The officials spotted the ball at that point. But as Bob trotted off the field, Bill Johnson, then the Bengal line coach, ran up and told him to get after the officials and tell them a fumbled lateral could not be advanced past the spot where it was recovered.

"I ran back out and I told the officials they couldn't advance a lateral but I really didn't understand what Bill was talking about," Johnson recalls. "The officials shooed me off the field and nothing happened. But Bill was right. I didn't know the rule but had I known it, I think I could have convinced the officials that they had made a mistake. It is very important for a captain to know what is going on in a game."

That even includes the toss of the coin before a game.

Bob has taken part in hundreds of coin tosses and many times has seen total confusion by the opposing captain if Johnson's call has been correct. In professional football, a team winning the coin toss always elects to receive but Bob recalls times when the other captain didn't know which way the wind was blowing or what goal to defend once that became his option.

"That is ridiculous," he says flatly. "It's a captain's responsibility when he walks to the center of the field to know exactly what he will do if he wins or loses the toss. He should get with his kicker and his coach and decide what options they want should his team have to kick off;

and know what their options will be as far as wind is concerned once the game enters the fourth quarter. That is part of being under control and being poised, something expected of every captain."

So, he adds, is having the dogged determination to play the game no matter what private circumstances might prevent the player, captain or not, from being at his best. For a younger player, it could be that his mother or father may be upset with him over something at home, but he should put that aside at practice or in a game and do the job expected.

Bob well remembers his senior year in high school when some college scouts were going to be at one of his team's practice sessions. But before he could go his father insisted that he cut the grass, a regular chore, even though it was a four-hour job. That came first, and though Bob certainly was tired he found no excuse or reason not to play well.

But the two incidents he remembers most vividly occurred during his professional career. One involved Tom DeLeone, a center for the Cleveland Browns. His wife died the day before a game but he played because she had told him that regardless of what happened to her, he had to play and play well. And during the middle of the 1976 season, Bob's own father passed away. It was a tragic blow to him but it did not deter him from playing and putting forth as much physical and emotional effort as he could.

"I was able to do it," he says, "because one of the

43

great lessons I learned from my father was that anything I did in my life required my total concentration, a fully conscientious effort, and proper physical preparation. He always told me that it didn't matter whether or not I was the team captain. If I applied those principles, then I never need be ashamed of winning or losing. That goes whether you're captain of a Midget League team or the Cincinnati Bengals."

PHOTOGRAPH BY FOCUS ON SPORTS

BOB LANIER

If there is one professional athlete who knows all that goes with the job of being a team captain it is Bob Lanier of the Detroit Pistons basketball team. Bob has been the captain for only a few years, but during that time he has endured every conceivable situation that any captain ever could face. His experiences have ranged from coaching changes to battles in the clubhouse to the calm and contentment when all is going well. He has been exposed to as many different types of personalities as there are players on the team, from those who are totally dedicated to playing to one who continually seemed to stumble over his every action.

Bob might not have surmounted all these problems and worked to rally his players had he himself not over-come personal difficulties that jeopardized his own

47

career. In the 1975 season, for example, he suffered two sprained ankles, a broken left collarbone, a cervical spine injury, two cases of flu, and tendonitis in both knees and his left elbow. And in that season, he still became the dominant NBA center for the last third of the schedule.

The collarbone was broken on January 3 but fifteen days later he was back in the starting lineup. Even though he was ineffective, his presence gave a psychological lift to his team.

"I thought maybe I could do something to help us," he said at the time. "I thought maybe I could make somebody guard me or something like that. I just wanted to try."

Ray Scott, then his coach, said he almost cried for Bob the last part of that season because of the pain he went through to put the Pistons into the NBA playoffs. It was because so much was expected of Lanier that he felt he had to play, even though doctors said the same condition in a normal athlete would have put him out for an entire season.

That summer, after a series of consultations with specialists, it was decided that Lanier needed to build the muscles around his damaged knee. His work and feats of strength in that rebuilding program still bring words like "unbelievable . . . astounding . . . amazing" from those on the Pistons.

"Bob played havoc with the weight machines all summer," says one of the team's medical staff. "We kept purchasing equipment because Bob kept extending the limits of the machines beyond their capacity."

Before he ever joined the Pistons after an all-America career at St. Bonaventure University in Olean, New York, he had to undergo massive knee surgery. Ironically, he injured himself in an NCAA playoff game when he tripped over Chris Ford of Villanova. Ford now is one of Lanier's teammates, a co-captain and a very good friend.

At the time, though, his career was in jeopardy because recovery from any kind of knee surgery is a tough situation. So much stress is placed on a basketball player's knees—because of the constant pounding on an inflexible hardwood floor—that a strengthening process is mandatory. With surgery as severe as Lanier was forced to undergo, that recovery time was slow and tremendously painful.

It so hampered him, in fact, that he had no lateral movement, and that is something that takes the heart from the game of any NBA center. He really played on one leg during that first season, and with the constricted movement never shed the excess weight that accumulated while he was unable to exercise during his knee's healing process. Some people labeled him lazy because of his limited movement; others said he never would become a good NBA center; and, in fact, even Lanier had problems proving his critics wrong.

"I was called a 'million-dollar bum' and other such uncomplimentary phrases," Lanier remembers from his rookie season. "That kind of stuff hurt."

After an intensive physical rehabilitation program the next season, he became a deadly hook shooter, using his six feet, eleven inches and 255 pounds to overpower other centers. Where he hobbled up and down the court as a rookie, he sprinted from end to end in his second year and began to dominate the backboards at both ends, to a point where he long has been the team's all-time rebounder.

"I'm not a naturally gifted jumper so I must move laterally to get into position to rebound and shoot," he says. "As a rookie, I had no movement at all. Once the knee was totally mended I got back on my game. That means playing offense *and* defense and it is the defense that I enjoy so much."

That is a significant statement because playing defense in professional basketball, or on any level for that matter, is an all-work, no-glory proposition. It means total concentration, being unselfish, and constantly working to help another teammate; it is an effort that often goes unnoticed because such things do not show up in a boxscore.

But Lanier is well known because he has been the team's top scorer and rebounder for nearly every season he has played in Detroit, and has the reputation of being the best outside shooter among pro basketball's big men. He has played in many all-star games and won the most valuable player award in the 1974 game when he scored 24 points and grabbed ten rebounds in just 26 minutes of play.

In the only one-on-one contest conducted among NBA players, he won the competition, beating the so-called quick, agile little men. He has scored more than 10,000 points in his career and predicts he'll finish among the top five scorers of all time when his career finally ends.

He has been the team's captain a short time, but he deserves his leadership position if you look at all he has accomplished since joining the Pistons in 1970. Being captain was not a job he really enjoyed when it was first given to him. A coach he truly liked, Earl Lloyd, was replaced by Ray Scott, a man he didn't particularly appreciate until he got to know him better. Yet he took the job for the good of the team.

Dave Bing, his roommate when the Pistons were on the road, had been the team captain before being traded. Bing and Lanier were close friends and Bob was hurt and disappointed that the team let him go. More than that, he had tremendous admiration for Bing's skills as a player and team captain, often marveling at how well he could handle both jobs without allowing one to affect the other.

"Dave was always bubbling, he was always there when you needed him, ready to help, ready with a good word, or with a well-thought-out word of advice that would help you be better," Lanier remembers. "He had a great way of making a person feel comfortable around him. There never were any temper tantrums, no displays of petulance, no airs that he had every right to put on because he truly was a great player.

"In the locker room, at practice or in a game, he always was level-headed. He came to do the job every night and I don't care who the player is, that is almost impossible. Yet David was always there. You could depend on him, and after I got my leg mended and began playing all-out, he and I depended on each other. The game became fun with him around."

Seeing his friend and captain traded weren't the only things that caused Lanier to dislike the job. There was turmoil on the team and he had the feeling that both the players and the management wanted him to be captain so each could use him for their own purposes. Still, he took the job.

"I told everyone, 'I'll wear the C for captain, but remember, it rips off, it is never permanent. Nothing is going to change with me,'" he says, adding: "I told them making me the captain doesn't automatically mean that everyone is going to come to me and I'll make everyone happy. I really didn't even know if I could be a captain because I equated the job with being like Dave Bing and I always had told myself I never could be like him or do the things that he did. I just wasn't built that way, mentally or emotionally."

But Bob Lanier always has been a man of great pride, willing to help when called upon, "The big brother, the ear that will listen, the spot to lean on," he says. Comparing himself, at first, with Bing's ability as team captain, Lanier was unsure of his own attributes. He doesn't consider himself a very aggressive or outgoing person. You won't find him jumping up and down with enthusiasm, though deep within his soul it is there, perhaps manifesting itself in a broad smile or in his eyes, which glow with pride when he is achieving all that he envisions for himself, in a game or in a season.

Still, there have been times since being named captain that he has become totally discouraged with some of the problems which have beset his team. He has even been on the verge of telling the Piston management to find another player for the job. But he never has.

"I remember one night," Lanier says, "when I was sick physically and had all the team hassles on my mind when the coach came up, smacked me real hard and said, 'Get 'em up, Bob.' All I could think about at that moment was, 'Well, who the heck is going to get me up after I get them up?' Those are the times when you must forget about yourself, reach back and do the job. You know it is important that you get those players up and not let them see you down. If they do, they'll never get up."

Sometimes he even kids about not wanting to be captain, noting, "Then I wouldn't have to practice every day." That is his particular way of ridding himself of the physical pain that often dogs his every effort. It is that way during a game too, when he still refuses to sit down because of a chronically sore back or tendonitis in his knees, or other aches and pains that NBA players accumulate during a season.

"I realize that my performance, especially at the start of the game, has to affect other people on our team," Bob says. "That's why I go so hard, why I can't sit down or

53

take a night off and Lord knows, there are times when I dearly wish I could.

"In a game, if I'm not shooting well, I can make up for it on hustle, or by hitting the boards or looking for the open man."

There was a game during the 1976 season against Bill Walton and the Portland Trail Blazers when Lanier missed his first four shots and spent the rest of the first quarter away from the basket, doing other things to help his teammates. ("After I missed those early shots I was looking to pass rather than shoot. I just wanted to get into the flow of the game.") It wasn't until the second quarter that he got into that flow and scored 13 points. He finished with 40 points, 13 rebounds, nine assists, four steals, two blocked shots, and held Walton to 14 points, only six in the first three quarters.

This shows his great regard for team play and for supplying the leadership by example that he knows will keep the other players working up to their capabilities. It also shows he is very conscientious in what he does: though he may not always relish the position, he still takes his job of being captain and team leader most seriously. It is when someone doesn't approach a game or play with the intensity which he can muster that he is frustrated. Often that frustration manifests itself in some natural discouragement, but deep inside is the spark that rekindles his spirit. It is this spirit that will always prevent him from ever shrugging off the responsibilities of being the Pistons' captain. He knows that he has the job for some very special reasons and he knows too that he cannot do it all by himself.

"The title 'captain' means nothing in itself," he says quite frankly. "I've played with people who were not great physical specimens, but they could have been midgets and people would have followed them. I never knew what particular characteristic they had, but it was there. The first time they opened their mouths to speak, you knew there was something special about them.

"I think much of it depends on who you are talking to. I've been in situations where no one gave a hoot what I said and I've been in situations where people have listened and genuinely tried to do what I asked.

"That's when I learned that you must depend on other people to be successful," Bob adds. "Considering the physical stress that professional basketball players must undergo with the travel and the schedule—sometimes we'll play five games in seven nights and travel from Detroit to the West Coast, and then from Seattle to Phoenix, and then back to Detroit to do it—there must be at least eight people on a team who have faith in each other. Those are the eight you know will come to play every night, regardless of how tired they are or how tough or easy the competition.

"You know they may not have the same intensity every night—no one does—but you know they'll be like a race horse. At the starting gate, everyone has faith that his particular horse is trying to go all out and trying to win the race. If you don't, then you're dead.

"But that's the key to anybody's success. We've had that kind of togetherness; we lost it for a bit, and we have it back again. When I first became captain, we had people on our team who really related to each other, players like Don Adams, John Mengelt, Chris Ford. We talked basketball all the time, and when we weren't talking basketball we were just sitting around together.

"We'd go to movies together, we'd go out and eat together, we'd laugh together and we'd get each other out of the doldrums together. Some of those players were traded and we had to start all over. That was tough on me personally because they were my friends. I had gotten so close to them and then they were gone."

At one point, Lanier promised himself that he never would get close to his fellow players again, that the hurt at seeing them leave was too much. But there is an inner quality within Lanier that overcame this emotional reaction, and soon he had started a series of togetherness sessions where the players would go out for some pizza after practice or a game and get to know each other better.

"Nothing too fancy," he says. "It doesn't have to be because all you really want is for everyone to sit down with each other and try to learn a little bit more about the other guy. If you begin to know something about a person and then like him, you'll want to play hard to help him."

Lanier is aware that not everyone on a team becomes instant buddies, that the togetherness which helps blend winning teams takes time and effort to grab hold. He knows most of all that this never will come about should cliques be allowed to develop. When his St. Bonaventure team was one of the nation's best during his collegiate days, the fruits of togetherness were reflected in its performances. Bob never has forgotten that feeling or the effects and he has tried to build the same thing on the Pistons.

"When the 1977 training camp started, we worked to develop a positive attitude, forgetting the problems we had in previous seasons," he says. "Situations caused some people to lose their tempers, to say things they really didn't mean and do things that were out of their control. No one really gets anywhere with attitudes like that. I remember when I was fourteen or fifteen years old, I really was high-strung. At the drop of a hat, I was ready to go at somebody and I really didn't change until my college coach, Larry Wiese, got me straightened around.

"He convinced me that in college basketball, you've got to keep yourself under control. There are teams who will try to goad you into a fight so you'll get tossed out of the game. If that happens, Larry said, what about your own team? A college team doesn't have great talent depth so if the best player goes, it makes it that much easier for the other team.

"Then Earl Lloyd, my second Piston coach, got me thinking about discipline, coming to practice on time, thinking about the good of the squad ahead of myself. He convinced me about the necessity of being prepared to play my best. Ray Scott, once I really got to know him

57

and to understand what he was trying to teach me, convinced me that I should be proud of who I was and who the Pistons were.

"People used to laugh at us, call us 'pigs in a poke' and other disparaging names. But Ray told us that we should have pride in what we do, in what we are, because there aren't many people in the world who are able to do it and do it as well. He helped make us proud to wear the Piston uniform and to think well of ourselves as professionals.

"All of this adds up to unity. If every player keeps himself under control, prepares himself thoroughly, takes pride in what he does, and tries to do his best, then a team is together. The captain is the one who must be out front and be a total part of this effort."

Sometimes, the captain also must be willing to go to the player who is not a part of this effort and try to obtain his cooperation. Lanier has faced this problem with a player named Marvin Barnes, a superbly talented athlete who never has disciplined his life to comply with whatever rules or restraints are placed upon him. His problem is that he is willing to listen to everyone and be responsive to no one.

When still a Piston, he sometimes would go to Lanier for advice on how to be a better team player. Lanier patiently explained what he felt was necessary and Barnes nodded his head as if he understood and would comply. Yet five minutes later, Bob would see all of his effort and his advice gone for naught.

"It upsets me because Marvin is a good kid and has the potential to be a fine person," Lanier says. "I just couldn't get inside his head and get him to understand what life really is about. All I did was to try and be responsive to him when he asked me. Maybe someday everything will come together for him."

There is another Detroit player who is highly emotional. Lanier has found that to argue with the man is useless because he strays farther and farther from logic. However, if he ignores the player and pays no attention to his tantrums, he'll come around and be responsive.

"Sometimes," Bob says with a smile, "a captain has to be a preacher, lawyer, psychologist—you name it. He's got to play many different roles just to get some idea of what is going on in the minds of his teammates. But if that's what the job requires and if you really care what happens to your team, you must do it.

"It's not all hard work, either. Take Leon Douglass. He's a young player who has everything that I'd love to have. His knees are sound, his back is sound, he's big and mobile. I enjoy working with him and trying to help him the way I wish someone had worked with me when I was a young pro. That is where some of the satisfaction comes with this job. I try and help a young player, and if he responds he becomes better and the team does better."

Lanier carries this spirit over into the locker room and has made extraordinary efforts to maintain a sound and solid relationship with his coach. Before a game, he'll talk to every player, sometimes needling his teammates, prepping their minds to do the job. Chris Ford remembers Lanier one night needling everyone he ran into, then going onto the floor and making his first seven shots and scoring 30 points in the game.

"You can see in the way he talks to you, with his little needles, just how intense he is about playing," Ford says. "When a player of his caliber gets this intense, you say to yourself, 'I'd better be ready too.'"

This leadership role is apparent to his coaches, particularly to Herb Brown, who succeeded Ray Scott and immediately stepped into a storm of controversy among some of his own players. It was this unsettled condition that caused Lanier so much anguish during the 1976 season. It reached a point one afternoon in Boston that after a practice he brought both sides together and demanded they stop the internal warfare.

And both sides did, at least on the surface. A sense of calm returned to the Pistons and they played with little outward discomfort the rest of the year. Brown was totally convinced that Lanier was the leader his club needed and though he appointed Ford as co-captain before the 1977 season began, placed great trust in Bob's decisions and experience. Though replaced as coach, he never regretted the decision.

Lanier worked to keep the Pistons together during turmoil. He defused any potentially dangerous racial overtones and tried to convince the players that Brown's methods of doing things were different from Ray Scott's methods because he was a different person. It was tough because Scott was well liked by his players and his displacement by management was not popular with them.

"All of our bickering was about unimportant things," Lanier says, "like players not getting enough playing time and wanting to be traded if they didn't get their own way. What bothered me was the waste of talent. We had more talent than any Piston team I could remember. My expectations were so high with all of that talent that I considered it a great waste that we should have been so caught up with such petty bickering. I've never felt any coach has an easy job, particularly one who coaches the Pistons. We have some hyper personalities, so some situations probably are blown out of proportion.

"When I think this is the case, I'll go to the coach and talk about it. I'm not afraid to tell him if I thought he mishandled a situation, and, perhaps, at the time he'll disagree with me. But there have been times too when he's come back and said I was correct. The big thing is that we do communicate, which to me is the lifeblood of my job. If I ever lose faith in what he is trying to accomplish, then I couldn't convey any kind of positive feelings to the players."

So Lanier and his coach win some and they lose some, but, regardless, they are together and so is the team. Bob does not like to play the go-between role where player and coach are involved. He prefers, if he has a complaint from a player, to tell his coach and then get the two parties together to straighten out the difficulty. Voice inflections or even facial expressions that say more than words can be lost when a third party carries messages back and forth. But if a player insists, then Bob will convey a message, but only because he feels it is part of his job as captain.

Oftentimes small things will rankle the players, such as not getting itineraries for trips, or the removal of a coffee machine from the locker room, or misunderstandings about the amount of meal money each player should get on road trips. In a tightly knit team situation, particularly one where strained feelings are trying to heal, these matters can become points of great contention.

A perceptive captain will see this and step into the breach. He will push to have some of the little things restored if he truly believes they will result in greater team harmony and concentration on playing the game. But the captain must know how to solve these problems so as to keep peace on both sides of the border and not alienate himself from either side. That is why Lanier feels that communication is the key to his remaining an effective captain; without it, he could not do the job.

All of this carries over to the playing floor. Here, Lanier is the leader, the motivator by example. He tries to carry his team along, to coax its momentum, and then work into a groove where everyone benefits. When he gets out of that groove, as sometimes happens, he knows there will be individuals who will come to him and say, "Don't worry, Bob. We'll keep it going until you get it together again."

Lanier says, "You really feel some sort of bond between yourself and other players when this happens, versus the guy who plays only for himself and really doesn't care what happens to you or the team. That's when you really want to go out and help a guy any way you can.

"I was working with Ralph Simpson one day. Because he is such a good shooter I couldn't understand why he was shooting so many 'bricks.' I told him either he was shooting the ball short because of not bending his legs or he was aiming for the front of the rim instead of the back. So the next day in practice I watched him and he was working on the two suggestions I made. I felt good watching him because I had made the effort to help someone be better and he was making the effort to be better himself."

Lanier is the same way off the basketball court. Maybe it is because he remembers his own youth in Buffalo, New York.

"When I was growing up, nobody took the time to teach me how to properly play basketball," he says. "It wasn't until I went to a boy's club in Buffalo that I was able to get started properly in fundamentals. I believe it's important for youngsters to have a good beginning. I hope kids who want to play basketball don't have to wait as long as I did to get good instruction."

That is why each summer he literally donates two weeks of his time to his basketball camp. It is why he also gives liberal amounts of time to youth work in the Detroit area, particularly among the disadvantaged. Perhaps, too, it is why his ex-coach, Larry Brown, says:

"He's a great player, the best I'll ever coach, but he's a greater human being. That is why he is the leader of the Detroit Pistons."

PHOTOGRAPH BY FOCUS ON SPORTS

SAL BANDO

There are few captains in professional sports better able to understand their role than Sal Bando of the Milwaukee Brewers. None have played under more diverse conditions than he; certainly none have encountered as many diverse personalities. During his first ten seasons in the big leagues, he played for just two teams—but for eight managers.

Eight managers! Anyone playing under that number generally is considered a journeyman, never good enough to stay in one place too long, or else a player whose problems exceed his ability.

Nothing could be further from the truth in Sal's case. He is considered a most stable player. He is talented enough to have been selected as an all-star third baseman three times. He played on the Oakland Athletics' three world championship teams as well as on the teams that won division titles five times. Not many major league players can match that record.

Perhaps Sal Bando's true worth is measured by what he has endured during such a glittering career. Most of that time was spent working for Charles O. Finley, owner first of the Kansas City and then the Oakland Athletics. Finley, to put it mildly, often was difficult to work for. He had his way of doing things and it didn't matter whether the manager was a winner or a champion, whether his players were all-stars or just good everyday performers. He scrapped with them all.

That's why Bando had so many managers. Until Dick Williams became Oakland's manager in 1971, Finley had a new manager for his team every year. What saved Williams was his ability to bring home a world championship three consecutive seasons, but after the third, even he had enough and resigned.

Through it all, Bando remained staunch. Though he played for so many different personalities, and under sometimes strained conditions, neither his playing ability nor his leadership capacity suffered. The proof? None of those managers ever said one negative word about either his playing or his leadership.

Neither did the Oakland players, whose personalities and talents were as diverse as the men who led them. This was a team of great talent—Joe Rudi, Reggie Jackson, Catfish Hunter, Rollie Fingers, Campy Campaneris,

Blue Moon Odom, Vida Blue, Paul Lindblad—good enough to win the world championship, good enough to become highly sought after whenever they offered their services as free agents.

There are true stories of fist fights in the locker room, shouting matches in the dugouts and team buses. Still, when these men walked onto the field, every personal animosity was forgotten and they worked to do only one thing: play winning baseball. Other teams have been ripped apart and their potential stripped from such activities.

Why it did not happen to Oakland is another tribute to Bando's leadership and ability to get players together. He was not then, nor is he now, a fiery leader, one who would go around indulging in his own muscle if players wouldn't shape up his way. Rather, his leadership is based on respect because of the way he went about his job and the manner in which he dealt with each player.

Billy North and Reggie Jackson had a well-publicized fight in the A's locker room a few years back, and it became a headline affair all over the country. The A's, after all, had become renowned for their openness in saying what they felt and about whom they felt it. Often it was about their owner, sometimes about each other. So when this little brush war broke into the open, player after player was interviewed and asked to replay the situation over and over. That made it even harder for the issue to die and threatened serious consequences to the team.

That this did not happen showed the strength of Bando's captaincy and the strong leadership from within the team. Neither Sal nor the other team leaders allowed themselves to be drawn personally into the matter, which could easily have formed sides and split the entire team wide open. As it was, the issue was smoothed over and the team continued on its way to another division title.

Bando looks back at that incident and at his term as the Oakland A's captain and sees it as "just another day on the job. When you played for the A's in those days, you really never quite knew what to expect from day to day," he says. "If anything, you knew never to get overly excited about any one thing because there might be something even more serious around the corner. I guess that was the single, most important quality that allowed all of us to survive during those years."

Perhaps the greatest indication of just how much respect Bando had generated was the manner in which the Milwaukee Brewers sought his services once he became a free agent after the 1976 season. Bando was in his early thirties then and certainly his playing time would not be for the long term. He signed a five-year contract, after which he felt his major league career would be ended.

This didn't faze Milwaukee owner Bud Selig. He saw Bando as the man who would help lead his team into contention for the first time.

"The first time I met Sal Bando was when he came to Milwaukee after the 1976 season," the Brewers' owner recalls. "Under baseball law, we couldn't discuss salary or contract terms but we did talk about a variety of things relating to our ball club. Four of us, including Sal, talked in my office for nearly five hours. When that meeting ended there was no doubt in my mind that he would be our top priority in the free-agent draft.

"It was so clear that he possessed those intangibles with which God blesses only a few of us," Selig continues. "There's a uniqueness about him that I haven't seen in many others. It's his quiet maturity and his dedication. He knows how to win and what it takes to win. That, in my thinking, is what an on-the-field leader should be."

It is easy for Sal Bando to focus on this approach. When he talks about the responsibilities of being a captain, the first point he makes is that anyone who must think about what a captain should do or how he should act probably should not be captain. To him, the position requires an inner quality that really has nothing to do with physical ability.

"Maybe it means being a bit more dedicated or a bit more aggressive or doing the right things on and off the field rather than being the person who can play better than anyone else," he says. "A person who must think about what the captain's role is about won't do a very good job because he always will be reacting to situations instead of creating them."

He just missed being captain of his baseball team at Arizona State University because he signed a major league contract with the Athletics. Had he stayed for his senior year, the job would have been his. As it was, four years later, in 1969, manager Hank Bauer appointed him captain of the Oakland Athletics.

"I remember my captaincy in high school," Sal says. He led the basketball and football teams. "At that time of a player's life, he often got the job because he was a better player than the others and played all-out, regardless of the situation.

"There are players who are considered the best but they don't play up to their capabilities all the time. The ones who have the capabilities and always give one hundred percent are the ones who make the best captains. Even in high school, it is necessary to understand the difference and to do something about it."

That "something" doesn't mean simply cheerleading or backslapping and allowing matters to end at that point. Regardless of where he played, Sal always took time to pat a teammate on the back when things weren't going well, and when they were he was among the first to shake hands for an important contribution.

It is important, he often has said, to understand that reinforcement is not restricted to the captain. It's called "picking each other up," and is something anyone on a team is capable of doing and should do, regardless of his status. It's what the A's did for each other during their championship years and what Bando tried to instill into the young players he joined in Milwaukee.

Sal was named the A's captain in only his second full season with the team.

"I was a little hesitant about accepting it because I had played only one full year in the big leagues," he says. "I thought some of the team's older players would resent it, but Hank Bauer, my manager, assured me there would be no resentment. He told me I was already doing the job of captain so I might as well have the title.

"What I did was never a conscious effort to be captain but came about because of how I approached playing every day. I was always in the game, not just to catch ground balls or to hit. I wasn't afraid to communicate with the other players or with my manager. During a game I always had made it a point to keep everyone informed on the various situations and I think this influenced Hank quite a bit in his decision."

From that time until the present, there never has been any feeling of discomfort on the part of his teammates. At Kansas City and Oakland, and later at Milwaukee, Bando said players felt no compunction about coming to him with whatever problems might be troubling them. They come to him either for advice or as a means of presenting their thoughts to the manager. Often they'll simply ask Sal to lay some groundwork for them so they can go in and speak for themselves. They know he will do it honestly and that their manager will give them total consideration because of Sal's willingness to speak in their behalf. That is respect, pure and simple.

It was respect that he earned, both from his fellow players and his managers. He never tried to usurp their authority, to downgrade their position, or do anything as team captain that would make them uncomfortable. Perhaps the most embarrassing moment of his career occurred in Oakland when Alvin Dark was the A's manager, following a tough, extra-inning loss to the Boston Red Sox.

Sal had been hitless in that game and had made the final out. As he walked into the team's clubhouse, he kicked a plastic trash can, being sure, he said, to find the biggest one around, and then blurted out in disgust and frustration:

"He [Dark] couldn't manage a meat market!"

He didn't realize that Dark was standing right behind him, along with two reporters ready to jot down what seemed to be more juicy bickering. Bando and Dark looked at each other, and immediately went into the manager's office to settle matters.

"As soon as we closed that door, Alvin asked me if I meant what I had said," Bando recalls. "There was no shouting or sense of bitterness in his tone because he just wasn't that way. I told him I didn't mean it personally. I had made the remark in a fit of anger, mostly at myself for messing up a good pitch and making the final out. I told Alvin I was sorry and repeated to him my firm belief that he was the boss who had the authority and that I would do whatever he said.

"We really cleared the air because things like that cannot be allowed to fester, particularly when the manager and captain are concerned. I knew the players were sitting out there wondering what would happen. They had every right to wonder whether or not he and I were fighting over who would control the team and then which side they would be on. Nothing like that ever happened and I let them know it.

"After that, we went out and won our next three games and everyone was saying, 'Boy, your little tiff with Dark really stirred things up and got the team moving.' Well, I didn't feel particularly relaxed and really felt quite badly about the whole incident. That wasn't my style. In fact, I put the man up against the wall and I didn't mean to do it. About the only thing it did was divert some attention being given to North and Jackson after their fight.

"But there was a lesson in what happened, even a lesson for someone who had played as long as I had and who had been in a leadership position for so long. I let down and thought only of myself. It was the wrong time and the wrong circumstance and perhaps with any other man than Alvin Dark, the consequences might have been much worse. It proved that when you are a team leader, you've got to be careful about what you say and when you say it. People expect more from you than kicking trash cans and making off-the-shoulder remarks that don't mean anything."

Bando has made it a rule throughout his major league captaincy never to take over the manager's role. Pete Rose, on the other hand, feels no restraint in saying something to his Cincinnati teammates whenever they make mental errors. Nothing rash, nothing harsh, but

73

something to remind them of what should have happened. He does it all within the limits agreed to with his own manager, but still he's so intense in his approach to the game that he feels it necessary.

But Sal Bando has always felt that discipline and the correction of mistakes were solely in the manager's domain.

"For one reason," he says, "who am I to correct someone when I might turn around and make the same mistake? The only exception might be when the game ended and if nothing ever was said about a particular mistake, I would go to the player and in a very nice way, point out what we should do the next time the same situation occurs.

"Players who care really don't resent honest criticism or having someone try and help them. I've had players come to me after a game and ask my opinions about our manager not having pinch hit, or played hit-and-run in certain situations. I never second-guessed the manager, regardless of whether or not I agreed with the player. I would try and explain what I felt the manager had in mind at the time. If I agreed with his decision, I'd add my own reasons for agreeing with him.

"But to second-guess the manager? Never! That's the easy part of the game and it's unfair to him. I've just never felt that because I'm the team captain I was better than anyone else or more capable of correcting things. During a game I always felt the responsibility of keeping everyone aware of the different situations but never of trying to infringe on a manager's prerogatives in running the game itself.

"It didn't take me long to find out that being the team captain doesn't exempt a person from having the same problems and frustrations as anyone else. At the same time, when you get down, you really can't hang your head. You can't afford to because you are the one player who should be setting the positive examples, or at least trying to. If it isn't part of his nature, it is something I strongly believe every captain should take great pains to achieve. I've always seen that to be a basic trait in players who are captains or team leaders."

Bando does not try to make something special of the terms "leader" or "leadership." In professional sports, he says, players should motivate themselves and strive to be as proficient as they possibly can. No matter how a player feels, or what the weather or field conditions, or who the opposing pitcher is, he should be playing his best. The captain should of course set an example.

"This is where you gain respect of your fellow players," he says. "I know too many good ballplayers who, if they have a headache, they don't play. That's not leadership and other players don't look up to them. The opposite really will be true. They'll figure, 'If he can't do it, why should I? He's the captain.' A captain, if he really takes his job seriously, must be a player who will give a team one hundred per cent, one hundred per cent of the time. If he won't or can't, then he should decline the post."

Bando remembers well his dealings with both Dick Williams and Chuck Tanner when they managed Oakland. Both were different in their approaches to the team and in what they gave in the way of leadership and motivation. Tanner was the better motivator because of the manner in which he dealt with his players. Williams was insistent on having things run his way, with little deviation. He might let a mistake go by once but if a player did it again or showed signs of being lackadaisical, he'd get on him. Some of the A's remember a game where one of the pitchers threw to the wrong base and Williams got after him for nearly fifteen minutes in the dugout while the game was in progress.

Tanner, on the other hand, went out of his way to give his players positive, yet aggressive, leadership. He knew that no one can go through a 162-game season and not have occasional letdowns.

"We could have been twenty games behind with twenty-one to play and he would say, 'We're going to win it,' and he'd still believe we would win," Bando remembers. "And if he didn't believe it, we'd never know it. There were days when he'd get us together in the clubhouse before a game and say, 'Look, I know you're tired. It's hot, you've got a doubleheader to play and I don't blame you for being tired. But let's go get 'em!' He was tired too, but he understood our problems. It was his positive attitude that gave us that little extra motivation. But the main job of motivation really is up to each man as a professional ballplayer.

"Dick Williams wasn't that vocal but he showed respect for you by the way he treated you. He recognized that each man was a veteran and that he had to be good or he wouldn't be in the big leagues. But that never kept him from correcting a player anytime he felt he needed it."

Bando's captaincy of the A's was probably unique. There were some very strong personalities in that organization, beginning with Finley, its owner; then there were players like Jackson, Hunter, Blue, Gene Tenace, and Rudi; and these players were managed by eight different men. Bando says much of what they said and did became like conditioned reflexes because they had lived with such turmoil for so long. Often they really were not conscious of what was happening.

It was not unusual for Finley to berate his players about their abilities or their mistakes. Once, he even called Bando "the worst-fielding third baseman in America," and Sal was his captain, expected to maintain a position of respect and leadership within the team. Perhaps a first instinct with anyone so maligned would be to fire back a bitter retort, but Bando checked himself.

"I just worked harder on my fielding, not to prove Mr. Finley wrong, but to prove that no one ever has to stop working at any phase of the game," he says. "In my last year with the A's, I think I fielded better than ever because Tanner and coach Al Monchak showed me how. Chuck got me moving when the pitch was made. I had heard about it before but no one ever showed me how.

He had me running in place, and then taking a step forward as the pitcher released the ball. No matter how long you've been playing, you simply cannot stop trying to learn and improve."

He approaches the art of hitting the same way. In Oakland he once fell into a batting slump and couldn't seem to work his way out. One day, he looked into the team's bat rack and found a couple of bats used by George Scott, then playing for Milwaukee. The bats had been given to his teammate Gene Tenace by Scott. They were longer and heavier than Bando's model but he decided to try them.

"They felt comfortable so I used one," he recalls. "The first time at the plate I hit a home run. Then in a period of seven games, I hit seven home runs. I don't say it was the bat, because hitting is really a psychological thing. Once you begin feeling you can hit, you generally do. It's a state of mind more than a matter of physical power.

"But again," he adds, "I had to do something at the time. I wasn't carrying my share of the load, and a leader, like anyone else, must be willing always to carry his share. Other players see you having problems and they'll watch to see what you do about them. If you sit back and try to wait them out, nothing much happens. But if they see you battling, even though you're a veteran or a team captain, it will encourage them to do the same. I never consciously thought about doing it because I was the captain, but, looking back, the qualities of wanting to make something positive happen are pretty apparent."

This was illustrated in a game against the Kansas City Royals. Joe Rudi had just laced a double that gave the A's a 3–0 lead, seemingly safe enough. Up came Bando, and on his own he laid down a bunt, trying to move Rudi to third base where he could easily score for a 4–0 lead. But that wasn't all. As he raced toward first base, Royals pitcher Al Fitzmorris tried to tag him with the ball. Sal knocked the ball from his glove and was safe.

"When I went to the plate, I simply wanted to get Rudi to third base," Bando recalls. "If I'd tried to get a hit off Fitzmorris, I would have tried to pull the ball and that doesn't always work out. Regardless, it would have taken a hit to move the runner from second, and I felt at the time the sacrifice bunt was the sure way to do the job."

Tanner says the significant thing about that play was Bando's willingness to give himself up. "Remember," the A's former manager points out, "Sal was in that tremendous home run streak. Whenever a hitter is going that well, his first instincts always are to go after every good pitch and get more. But Sal never was anything but a complete team player and he was willing to forgo the thrill of a home run for a sacrifice bunt. That was just one instance of his setting such a tremendous example for the other players."

Yet there were differences in being the captain of the Milwaukee Brewers and Oakland Athletics. If anything, his tenure with the A's was easier because his best friends also formed a nucleus of team leadership. They were the starters, men who played day after day. Bando didn't stand alone and anyone, particularly younger players and the substitutes, could easily see that the team leadership was strong and positive. Those who were its leaders were successful and made no bones about how the success was achieved. They worked at it.

In Milwaukee, he joined a comparatively young group of players who had never experienced, in the big leagues, any kind of long-lasting success. The Brewers' management expected Sal to provide the life and guidance these players needed. He was to do it by example, and through his talent and dedication.

Yet he didn't set out in his first spring training with the Brewers as a dedicated crusader. First, he did all he could on the field. Then, rather than buttonhole one player after another, he found it easier to impart some of his wisdom and experience in group discussion with a few players at a time. He'd give his opinions as to what he thought they could do to improve and what he felt were the proper ways to approach things and left it to them to understand and follow through. But he always tried to set a good example.

"There was nothing terribly mysterious about these get-togethers," he says. "They were spontaneous, usually at dinner on the road or sitting around in the clubhouse before or after a game. I think the big thing I tried to impress on the younger players was that baseball is not a job where you come to the ballpark for three hours and then forget about it. I told them a doctor doesn't become a good doctor because he spends three hours on a house call, nor does a lawyer become good because he spends three hours in court. There is more to it than that. I told them to be successful they've got to think more about what they're doing, they've got to analyze what's good and what's bad.

"No good professional comes to the park, plays, and then leaves. Playing professionally, regardless of the level, should be a full-time job. A player should prepare himself for every game just as the lawyer is prepared when he goes into court. And when he finishes, he should reflect on all that has happened and see where he can do better the next day. In that respect, playing baseball isn't too much different from anything else a person tries to accomplish in life."

This has been a sort of personal credo Bando has followed since his boyhood in Cleveland, Ohio, when he spent whatever spare moments he had watching the great Indian teams of the fifties, or playing baseball himself. Because he was the captain of his football and basketball teams in high school, he knows the difficulties young people face as well as those faced by veteran players.

"Regardless of whether it is high school or the big leagues, anyone who wants to be a team captain should be willing to stand up for what they think is right," he says. "They should do the best they can and not what they feel might be expected of them. It isn't always that important that a team captain lead in home runs or be the high scorer. A person can only do what his or her ability will let them do.

"Another point that I feel is most important at every level is to be your own person. Don't be afraid to look at another player and see what makes him something special. Is it because he gives one hundred per cent, or is it because he is just the best player? Or is it because he is always in the game and doing things right? That is a decision everyone should make for themselves.

"That's what it takes to be captain . . . that, and acting like a captain off the field. I feel very strongly about this point. A person's reputation off the field is just as important as it is on the field. In the big leagues, a captain who breaks the rules or isn't ready to play every day simply isn't going to be a good captain. It's the same anyplace. If you are a member of a team and there are rules, then you, as captain, must be the first to abide by every rule."

PHOTOGRAPH BY UNITED PRESS INTERNATIONAL

GEORGE KUNZ

George Kunz is a perfect example of a player whose name does not blaze in headlines each week but who has the qualities of an excellent team captain. This doesn't mean that George is not a very good player or that he is not well known. On the contrary, as an offensive tackle, he was an all-American player at Notre Dame and in the National Football League he has been selected as an all-pro tackle five times during his career with the Atlanta Falcons and Baltimore Colts. And in 1976 he was selected by all the other NFL players as the best blocking lineman in professional football.

George's career proves that a player need not be the team's superstar to have its respect and to carry on the function of being one of its leaders. Since joining the

Baltimore Colts, and getting his first captaincy in professional football, Kunz has been surrounded by strong, talented teammates. Certainly none is more dynamic than Bert Jones, the team's great young quarterback and one of its acknowledged stars. Lydell Mitchell, Baltimore's great running back, is another whose name and feats are well known.

But neither Jones nor Mitchell were chosen as offensive captain by their fellow players. Instead, it was a player whose job is in "the pits," the term describing the offensive linemen who must open the holes for the runners like Mitchell and protect passers like Jones. It is not very glamorous work because no one really watches or knows too much about what these men do or how they do it.

Nearly everyone watching a game will follow the ball from the moment it is snapped until the play ends. What they see may be runners like Mitchell driving through a huge hole in the line or a beautifully thrown pass being caught for a touchdown. The runner, the quarterback, and the receiver all get the cheers but no one has seen the classic confrontation of man against man in the line which made all of that possible.

Kunz and other good offensive linemen who take great pride in their performance and contribution to a team don't really mind. Their satisfaction comes from a job well done and the recognition they'll receive from their fellow players and coaches. They work as hard as anyone in athletics perfecting the skills which make them proficient, even though their work doesn't involve the glamour of throwing, running, and catching, which some actually think is everything in football.

Kunz will tell you there is much more to the game, just as there is much more to being a team captain than calling heads or tails at the flip of the coin before each game. That is why you will find captains on many teams who are not the superstars. There is no denying the superstars' ability to play but they may not be as capable of relating to the other players as those in less glamorous positions. Of course, that is not an unbreakable rule, because Bert Jones, for example, might make an excellent team captain just as Roger Staubach of the Dallas Cowboys, another quarterback, is the captain of his team.

"The big job of any captain is being able to communicate with his teammates and coaches and do it on a fair and honest basis," Kunz says. "There are players who, when they get into a game, are dynamic leaders. They can get a team going and keep it going, either with their play or by keeping every man alert. Yet, when there is no game, they go about their job of getting ready and see this as their most important function during a week-long preparation period."

Some professional football coaches feel, for example, that a quarterback will be the leader on the field during a game so the quarterback really doesn't need the title of captain. These coaches feel as well that the quarterback has so much to do during a week to prepare himself that he should not be distracted by the internal interruptions that concern a captain, and that the quarterback's relationships between himself and the players and himself and the coach should be kept spanking clean.

Kunz, a lineman, does not mind dealing with those relationships. "A major function of any team captain off the field is seeing to it that little problems don't become big ones. People sometimes must be told what must be done for the overall good of the team," Kunz says. "Much of that means relating to different people on different levels.

"The job really begins with acting as a liaison between the players and coaches. If a question comes up that bothers either side, then it is up to the team captain to find out what is happening and the reasoning behind any decisions that might be causing some question. Unless you can get an answer for them, then they can begin to think anything they wish, and quite often it will be the wrong thing. That can cause a problem.

"A successful captain must be able to talk to all of the players. He must be careful to see that cliques aren't forming on the team because that sort of thing just takes away from the overall goal of the team to be totally successful and, in the case of professional football, go to the Super Bowl and win. In any sport, a clique of players who work against the rest of the team can spoil that team's chances because they are not a total part of an effort to win.

"Of course, there is the emphasis on telling people what must be done, not necessarily because they want to hear it, but because you think it's important for the over-all good of the team. That could happen during a practice when things may go bad or individual efforts begin to slacken. If that occurs, then the captain should say to the ones who aren't going all out, 'Come on, pick it up. We've got to get going right now.' "

Like every other captain, George feels all of this can be done only if the captain himself is giving a full effort. He places great emphasis on what is accomplished during a team's practice, a point often overlooked because so much emphasis is placed on playing a game.

"You've got to get some good from your practice time and if you don't, then it's all a waste," he says. "If you waste time, then you don't perform well and you won't attain your final goal. And if you do try your best, others will notice and get the example. The harder people work in practice the better they become. It's that simple."

Kunz knows what he's talking about. When he played for the Atlanta Falcons, he used to work against Claude Humphrey, one of the NFL's best defensive ends. Kunz would work on his blocking techniques for pass plays and Humphrey would work on his pass rushing techniques. Each would try to beat the other; each would work at his best against the other. The result: each became superior in his own skill.

He carried that over to the Colts and works hard every day against Fred Cook, one of Baltimore's outstanding defensive ends.

"If I go against Freddie as tough as possible every day,

he will get better and I'll get better," Kunz says. "More than that begins to happen, too. Other players see us going hard against each other—not to hurt one another—but as we would in a game and that example carries over to them. Each player on the offense begins to work hard against the player on the defense, each using his skills to the utmost. This is what ultimately builds a successful team because each of us is helping the other to improve."

He is absolutely correct, and if you look at any successful team over a period of years you'll find that was always its habit. The players came together as a team because they were willing to help one another, to pick up one another if times got tough during a game or in a crisis, to share equally the good and bad moments. The Minnesota Vikings, for example, had a motto the season they won their first NFL title and went to the Super Bowl. It was "40 for one." Later that year when Joe Kapp, then their quarterback, was presented a trophy as the league's most valuable player, he refused to accept it, saying that it belonged to the entire team.

On the Colts, Kunz and the other offensive captain, tight end Raymond Chester, see their team receive tremendous leadership from quarterback Bert Jones. This is a case of where a team has a very strong leader in its quarterback and also strong leadership from the captains. Sometimes their roles cross; many times they do not.

"Bert's responsibility is the eleven men working together," Kunz points out. "My responsibility is to help him reinforce that function. Normally, all of us refer to the quarterback as the field general. Then the captain should be the staff sergeant, the man who keeps things pulled together and helps the quarterback implement what he wants to do. The quarterback has studied our game plan a lot harder than I have and he knows what he wants to do. That is his realm of responsibility. Mine is to get people to realize what he wants to do and get them to do it.

"If things aren't going too well, if people are breaking down, or if we get behind quickly, I'll get with the offensive guys and tell them, 'Okay, let's just get out there and do our jobs. If we can't do that, then we don't deserve to win.' The key is to reaffirm what we should be doing, regardless of the situation, and get our attitude toward winning back on the right track. If you have a group of players who have worked hard all week to prepare for that goal, then it doesn't take much to help them get squared away. That's the way it has been on the Colts since I came."

George can recall a game against Navy during his days at Notre Dame when a teammate named Jim Reilly, who was playing left tackle, asked him a question on the field and didn't get an answer, but only because Kunz didn't hear him. Reilly thought he was being ignored and lost his temper. In a moment, the two men almost came to blows, though each was playing an excellent game.

"When we came to the sidelines, all the other offensive linemen were looking at us, wondering if we were going to punch each other out," Kunz recalls. "I went over to him and said, 'Jim, if there's a misunderstanding, I'm sorry. Now let's get back to the business at hand and play the game.' Everyone walked away and we straightened out the problem.

"But it could have blown up and gotten out of all proportion unless we got with each other immediately. I made a mistake as the team captain but I had to downplay that mistake. A captain is human and he can make a mistake and no one should hold it against him. At the same time, he must realize the other players are human too and not get so intense over something that bickering is the result. But in the end, as the captain, he must be willing and able to straighten out those misunderstandings and get everyone back to playing all out."

Like anything else, much of this is learned by experience. Though George was captain of his college team, when he became one of the Colt captains he had to discover for himself exactly what his role was. In the end, through some trial and error, he found it was nothing more than being himself and trying to give as much of himself to the needs of the other players as possible. The key: being himself.

"When a team elects you as its captain or a coach appoints you to the job, you already know the reason is because your leadership is needed," Kunz says. "By leading you really are being yourself and applying yourself to situations that you think are right. From that standpoint, anything you do really can't be wrong because the other players know you are giving it your best shot. So does the coach.

"There also are times when you might wonder if you really are doing enough, or if you are doing too much. Then you go and ask the players or ask the coach. You find out what they need, what they want and you find out too, what you want and what you need. Then you know the limits and anything you do will be within your own capacity."

If you listen to Kunz discuss his job as captain, you soon are aware that he takes its responsibilities very seriously. He has been through the so-called discovery process and he knows exactly what is expected of him. He knows that his responsibilities during a game are very important. A player not under control could blow his cool and cost the team a 15-yard penalty, which if it nullified a 40-yard gain on a pass, would be a very serious and costly mistake. Kunz must be sure that does not happen.

During a game, he works constantly at his own job of playing right tackle but is quick to step in and remind other players that they must keep their minds on their jobs and not worry about other things.

"An offensive player is different from the defensive guy," he says, "because the offensive guy must keep working, he can't want to stop. You really want to get tired because that means you've worked a long time and you should be scoring some points. The defense, on the other hand, hopes to go on the field, play three downs and come off again. So it takes a little bit more to motivate an offensive player and to keep him thinking constantly about how much he must work for a team to be successful. That is where the captain must keep the players aware and ready, not let them drag or get sloppy."

This definitely falls within the realm of leadership, of which, like any captain, Kunz has his own particular definition: "The act of wanting to display admirable qualities; of downplaying bad ones in the hope that another person would see the good points and want to follow the example."

One of his most admirable traits is his willingness to admit he is not a perfect human being, that he is capable of making mistakes but that he always will try to do his best.

"I may do things wrong," he notes, "and I am critical of myself in those times. People don't have to tell me. But a leader really wants to display enough good qualities so that others will want to follow his example.

"This is something I've thought a great deal about," he continues. "I don't think that leadership is something limited to a select number. Everyone can be a leader, in his or her own way. If you look back in history or in any area of endeavor, you'll find your great leaders were people who were able to overcome obstacles and were in a position for others to see their good points. What it boils down to is that your great leaders are the people who display more than average good qualities."

During his own career, starting at Loyola High School in Los Angeles, Kunz has seen many players and coaches who were excellent leaders. He recalls a Loyola teammate named Don Schwartz, who was captain of Loyola's team and later was the captain of Stanford University's football team.

"Don was a popular guy, for sure, but he also was a loner, a person who did a lot of things on his own," Kunz remembers. "But what made him a leader was his great ability to exude self-confidence. Yet he always took care to not overlook the little things. There was a track meet at Loyola one year and Don ran the half mile for his class against some other guys who were a lot lighter and probably a bit more adept at the sport. He was dead last coming into the final 220 yards but somehow he kicked in the stretch, won the race, and then collapsed when he crossed the finish line. What made him win was his determination not to be last, not to lose.

"I also think that my Notre Dame coach, Ara Parseghian, was probably one of the most dynamic leaders I ever have met. Rocky Bleier of the Pittsburgh Steelers and Jim Lynch, who played for Kansas City, were two other players at Notre Dame who were tremendous leaders."

From Parseghian he saw what rewards motivation, honesty, and hard work can reap against tough competition. Those three qualities, taken together, can make a person tougher mentally than his opponent and it is in the mind where many individual little battles are won. Along with great intelligence, Kunz says the secret of

Parseghian's success at Notre Dame, often against teams more talented, was forged from those qualities because he passed them on to each of his players.

Kunz remembers a game that Notre Dame played against Georgia Tech when Bleier suffered a severe leg injury in the first half that should have kept him out of the game in the final two quarters. Instead, he wound up gaining over one hundred yards. Bleier's actions as a soldier during the Vietnam war, during which he was wounded and almost lost his foot, qualify him as a leader as much as his feats at Notre Dame and with the Steelers qualify him as an athlete, George adds.

As a sophomore at Notre Dame, when Lynch was captain of the Fighting Irish national championship team, Kunz was injured during the second game of the season and did not play any more that year. Still, he would attend practices and visit the locker room. "Jim always had a good word, not necessarily for everybody but for people who needed it. He was the type of person who could demonstrate good qualities. In fact, I can't think of one bad one. Any he had he hid very well or he downplayed them."

Kunz remembers hearing Bill Russell, the former center of the Boston Celtics great championship teams whom many consider the greatest player in the sport's history, speak at a Notre Dame football pep rally. Russell, always a man of few words, told the assemblage, "There are two no more certain things in this world than Boston Celtics basketball and Notre Dame football."

"That's all he said," Kunz recalls. "Just one sentence, but that's all anybody needed because you could feel the charisma that he exuded as a leader. I felt at that moment those words were meant just for me and I'm sure every other person felt the message was just for him."

With the Colts Kunz definitely is a leader, but, as on any good team, Kunz knows he has help from a group of other players. Ray Chester, the other offensive captain, Ken Mendenhall, and Elmer Collett are a few, but the important thing for George is that he knows the capacities of leadership for every player he must deal with.

He knows that Collett is a gung-ho, go-get-'em aggressive guy who wants to do everything on the field. He knows that Mendenhall, the team's center, is a thinking man's player, who weighs and studies every situation carefully. He knows that Bob Pratt, a guard, enjoys the contact aspects and that young Dave Taylor is working hard to become a good offensive tackle because he utilizes his strong points and works to strengthen those areas which need help.

"What it boils down to," Kunz says, "is that I know what I can expect from these people. I never push them beyond it. As the leader, I really can't. I know what Lydell Mitchell can do and I don't ask him to do any more because it would be impossible. I know that they'll get down on themselves once in a while but I know how to get them working again, simply by knowing what to say to each man."

Bert Jones does it a bit differently. The team watched

him play for a season with ribs so badly cracked that he had to wear a protective cast around them during the games. Some quarterbacks would sit down with such an injury, but any player who thought he was hurting too badly to play and saw Jones moving through the agony of cracked ribs would forget his own miseries.

"A guy doesn't have to say anything with that kind of example," Kunz says. "Yet Bert never let on he was in pain. He played with his usual style, which is to do his job and keep up a constant stream of chatter that is meant to encourage us. That's his style; he's a bit of an on-the-field cheerleader who backs up his words with plenty of action. He talks to us, to the officials, even to the other team sometimes because that's his way of keeping himself and us in the game."

Kunz also has help from his coach, Ted Marchibroda. Both have discussed the limits of George's responsibility and, while Marchibroda has the reputation of being a firm coach, there is a great amount of respect for his captains and the job they must do.

"I know how far I can go, yet I know that if there comes a time when I might have to step a little farther than usual, I can do that and then step back and not have ruptured the feelings between Ted and myself," Kunz says. "He has been in pro football a lot longer than me, so I have great respect for his wisdom and experience. So does every man on our team, and because of that there are few times when such matters ever would get that serious."

There is little doubt about this. A few years ago when Robert Irsay, the team's owner, in a fit of anger forced Marchibroda to resign, the players refused to play until he was reinstated. The squabble mainly dealt with front office policies and obvious interference by Joe Thomas, then the team's general manager, into the coach's responsibilities. The force of the team leadership so shocked and impressed Irsay that Marchibroda was rehired within a couple of days and given fuller responsibility for handling the football operations of the team.

These developments created a healthy climate within the team and established the quality of its leadership. Marchibroda will listen to Kunz or the other Colt captains if they come to him with something they feel is a problem.

"Take the example of a well-liked player who is released," Kunz says. "Other players think a lot of his ability but they'll want to know if there was a personality conflict with the coach. They'll ask, 'What was the reason? If there was a problem why didn't they solve it sooner, or why wasn't he released sooner?' When I get those questions, I have to go to the coach and tell him there is a potential area of contention unless I can provide the answers. They may not like the answers but at least they'll know.

"We may go to Ted and tell him the practice field needs some work because guys are getting edgy about hurting themselves. Or we may ask him why some new rules were laid down. But we never will question his authority about such things as the length of practice, or the evaluation of a player, or what he does during a game.

"I have no right to infringe on that area and I wouldn't even try," Kunz says. "But little things that bother a club should be made known to the coach because he may not even be aware of them. The little things can grow into big things and become like an open sore that will become infected and cause problems. If you take care of that sore right away, clean it up, apply some antiseptic, then you avoid a permanent injury or a scar. That's a captain's job—avoiding the little nicks that could ultimately scar a team."

Being the captain of his team at Notre Dame was excellent preparation for being captain of the Baltimore Colts and the only real difference is that George no longer has to attend classes or maintain a prescribed grade level. Yet at Notre Dame, he had to keep open the lines of communication between the team and Coach Parseghian. Both parties gave this matter full attention.

"Coach Parseghian was an easy man to approach and he wanted to know what was going on," Kunz says. "Let's say, for example, that somebody got in trouble off the campus, which happened rarely when I was in school. I'd check out the situation with the coach and if he had any questions, I'd try to find out the facts, present the player's side, and then come up with a disciplinary action to fit the wrongdoing. He was always open to suggestion, very fair, and would take our advice and use it along with his own experience to arrive at a final decision."

Many probably find it surprising that a coach would accept recommendations from one of his players for disciplinary action against another player; or even that a team captain would go so far as to recommend that a fellow player be punished. But all of that is part of being a leader and being expected to step out front and deal with other players in a positive manner. It is one reason why the best player doesn't always make the best captain because he might not have the capacity for such actions.

Kunz recognizes that young people sometimes feel they must follow the most popular player, thinking that the player "is my friend, I want to be close to him. Therefore let him be the team captain and I will be close to him."

"That is false," George says emphatically. "Sometimes it can work either way. If a guy is a popular guy and he doesn't work hard, then the team doesn't work hard and no one is successful. The reason a person should be chosen as team captain is because he's supposed to be a little taller in some levels—not necessarily in height—than other people. If he's not, then he shouldn't be there. Let the person who can demonstrate that trait be the captain.

"If a person wonders, 'How will I recognize such a person?' or 'Am I capable of doing that job?' all you need do is be yourself. Work on what you consider to be good traits. If you make a mistake, admit it. Don't play up mistakes. Play up the good point. Play up what you think other people would like to emulate.

"If it's a bad quality, then you're not going to fool anybody, other than yourself. Try to emphasize good points, don't try to be all things to all people. Be yourself, and try to contribute. Try to give back more than you take. It's that simple."

PHOTOGRAPH BY FOCUS ON SPORTS

BOBBY CLARKE

During the 1972–73 season, Fred Shero, the new coach of the National Hockey League's Philadelphia Flyers, appointed Bobby Clarke as his team's captain. Since then he has seen him working and playing under every imaginable circumstance, including two Stanley Cup championships and countless other playoff games. So when Shero talks about Bobby Clarke, as a hockey player, team captain, and as a person, you must listen and pay attention.

"If Bobby Clarke was a sewer digger in Flin Flon, he'd be the best sewer digger and the hardest worker. You cannot say that of other athletes or captains," Shero says without hesitation.

Even reading between the lines that is heady praise,

particularly coming from Shero, a person who has made a life-long study of the reasons why people—himself included—achieve success. Obviously, he feels that Clarke is the best possible player he could have selected to be captain of the Flyers and, for that matter, of any other team he ever would coach.

While everyone may have a favorite hockey player, it is difficult to dispute Shero's estimation of his own captain because the records back him up. Talentwise, many consider Bobby to be the best all-around player in professional hockey. He is a magnificent playmaker, always among the league's leaders in assists, which shows too that he is totally unselfish because he is talented enough to be among the NHL's top goal scorers. As a center iceman, he has no peer on defense, often getting the job of guarding the opposition's best scoring center. He does all of this though he is a diabetic, which demands rigid control of his diet as well as a daily intake of insulin serum that allows his system to function normally.

That he can play professional hockey, let alone play it so well, is a bit amazing too, considering the physical demands on his body. If Clarke or any other hockey player plays two full minutes at a time skating at top speed, passing or shooting the puck, backchecking and forechecking, and making bodily contact with other players, the exertion is tremendous. Legs become like rubber, lungs gasp for air. Ask anyone who simply ice skates at top speed for that length of time without the physical strain of playing hockey.

But Clarke is more than a good skater or an excellent

hockey player. He has the attributes within his own person to be a leader, to demand of himself, his coaches, and fellow players that they give their best at all times. He is not afraid to speak up to a teammate if he feels the man is not playing as he should. He's done that, many times and without taking into account who the player is and what he has achieved. He has challenged Shero, during a game and during a practice, if he feels his coach is not getting the most from the team. And he is not afraid to challenge the team's management if he feels it is not being fair to the players.

All of this from a young man who was as surprised as anyone on the Flyers when Shero named him as captain early in the 1972 season. He replaced a popular veteran, Ed Van Impe, who remained to play with the team and played well, and with whom Bobby never had a problem, before or since. Even so, Clarke really didn't want the job because he felt he was too young and lacked the NHL experience to become a good player and at the same time take on the responsibilities that went with his captaincy.

All of this didn't bother Shero. He has always maintained that a good captain need not be the most talented player, though now Bobby is both. But he does insist that in the forty or so years he has been involved with hockey teams he never has seen a *good* team captain who has not been an outstanding person. It took him a full training camp and one month's play to see that Bobby Clarke was his man.

"If I was still playing," Shero says, "I'd give half of my

salary to play on the same team with Bobby Clarke. He's the most valuable player I've ever seen in any sport. He also is the perfect captain. He does so much to make our team what it is. I never had a team with so much courage, discipline, and spirit. And most of it comes from Clarke."

That is why Shero's selection process was not that difficult. He had his own set of standards and he knew the kind of player he did *not* want to be his captain. He did not want to inherit a player from another coaching regime or selection process. He did not want one who would be the favorite of management "because there's no way they're going to help you." Nor did he want a man selected only by the players "because they want a guy who's just for them and not for management."

"I've entered situations like that," Shero adds, "and until I've corrected them and eliminated that captain— even though he was a fine person—the team was not successful. When I joined the Flyers, Ed Van Impe was the captain and a fine person but I felt I needed a guy like Clarke.

"I could see the good discipline in his life and the dedication that he showed for his job," Shero says. "I could see that even at his young age [twenty-three] he wanted things done right in our drills. He resented the times when the older players might be taking things too lightly. All of these leadership qualities were so evident, and I see no reason to make a man wait until he's thirty or forty years of age to make him a captain. Not if he is ready for the job."

108

Actually, Shero places no age limit on being a captain. Having studied at great depth the reasons why teams and people are successful, and why they are not, he says that in any group of ten or twenty people, there are always a couple of natural leaders, whether they realize it or not. It doesn't happen only in professional sports but even with teams whose players may be no more than ten years old.

"I've found that youngsters at that age automatically look to a leader," he points out. "There is somebody in every group of kids who is a leader. He is the one who organizes the games, who demands fair play, who demands that in choosing sides each team be fairly and evenly selected for talent. He's not the guy who is always trying to get the best player for himself. Later in life, those are the people who become the natural captains. And if I check back and see that those boys never went any further in athletics, I've found they are very happy no matter what work they're doing. They're happy people in marriage and everything in their life is beautiful."

Being a team captain is not new to Bobby. He had the job with his junior hockey team in Canada, but it didn't take him long after reaching the NHL to discover there was a world of difference between a junior hockey captaincy and one in the NHL. Players on his junior hockey team were in their teens and their interests were divided among playing hockey, girlfriends, and parties. The coach ran the entire show, including the selection of the captain.

"That's the only way to have it," Bobby insists. "At that level, if you leave it up to the players, you end up with personality conflicts. Some guys are going to be mad because somebody didn't vote for them. Really, there is little authority vested in the captain because the coach has to insist on a great deal more discipline and be a lot tougher on the young kids than on guys making a big salary in the NHL.

"But when you become a captain in the NHL, you have to be careful. Players are being paid a lot of money to be good hockey players and some of them don't like being told what to do."

For a young player, that can be a dilemma. He can get the job and keep it without doing too much, figuring he won't make anyone mad, or at least he'll take it easy until he finds out what the job is all about. Or he can immediately begin acting like a captain. Shero says Bobby Clarke didn't hesitate at all.

"I knew he was going to be good but I never knew he would be *that* good," the Flyers coach says. "One thing I liked about him right away was he would not be a yes man. I don't like those kind in my organization. I want someone who, if he is not sure what I say is right, will speak right out and tell me so, at any moment, at any time, even during the course of a game. I want that man to say, 'This is not right.' Sometimes I deliberately do something wrong just to see who has the courage to speak up.

"I've had other captains who would feel I was wrong

but they might wait a couple of weeks before they got up enough courage to say something about it. Bobby had the courage immediately and he also never hesitated to speak against management if he felt it was wrong. I've never known a person in sports to do that at the outset of his captaincy."

Shero, by appointing Clarke rather than holding an election, made the captain's job a bit less pressurized because the players realized their coach had made the selection and that he had vested Bobby with full authority. In so doing, Shero made it clear that any captain, Bobby Clarke or someone else, had to participate fully as a team member, though he need not be the best player. That removed the tarnish of the star system and showed the players there were other qualities and responsibilities that went with the job.

The foremost was not what Clarke did on the ice but what he did off the ice. Shero says the real leadership on a team is in this area, that teams with good talent which do not win are failures because there is no leadership on or off the ice.

"The coach can't be with the players day and night," he says. "My captain, in this instance Bobby Clarke, has to be a leader during the times I'm not around. He's got to be the go-between for the players and management. He can't be only for the players but must realize that management also has some rights.

"I've found that on any successful team the captain is an outstanding person, regardless of the sport. I don't care what he does later on in life, he will be a success because he will do his job better than anyone else. Bobby Clarke has fit that mold, in my estimation."

Obviously, Shero places great faith in the work of Bobby. He doesn't hesitate to place as much responsibility as possible on Bobby's shoulders because he knows the job will be done properly. He knows that in those instances when he isn't around, his captain will keep control, that he will come to the coach when there are problems that can hurt a team if allowed to go unnoticed; Shero also knows that a good captain can smooth over rough edges himself.

"Team captains are so important and I don't think they're given enough credit for the jobs they must do," Shero adds.

At this point in his career, though, Clarke does not see himself as a great team captain nor does he feel his captaincy has a make-or-break quality, because the Flyers are an experienced and established team that has proven its worth and is highly motivated toward success. He feels all leadership should be by example, something that is natural for him, not by screaming or shouting. Consequently, each of his teammates knows that if he is to keep Clarke's esteem, he'll have to follow his example.

He places little credence in the fact that the Flyers didn't begin to vie for championships until Shero became coach and he became captain. Yet that was the case. Clarke says the team got better because it was on the rise and would have reached championship status, regardless of his captaincy. Other teammates say that Bobby set the standard every day, every game, and that combined with Shero's astute coaching, the Flyers became better much faster than even they thought possible.

"I think it is important for any captain to get a good grasp of what his role really is about," Clarke points out. "The big thing is to set an example. I don't think anyone on a team expects the captain to be the biggest eater, or drinker, or party-boy. Nor do I think a good captain would break curfews or the rules that the club has laid down. On the ice, I don't play any harder because I'm the captain than I did before I got the job. Being captain hasn't made me a better player, but as a captain, you hope your example may make someone else better."

Yet Bobby acknowledges special times when it takes more than good example to get his team going. Some players are capable of knowing when these times are but don't have the talent to do much about it. It's up to the ones with talent to show the way, and that generally means the team captain.

"I've been in games where we really have been struggling and not getting anywhere," Bobby says. "I don't often fight on the ice but maybe I'll get involved and that seems to get the other players stirred up. Or maybe there are times when I'll get the all-important goal to break a tie or bring us even, something that gets us going."

Sometimes there are cases where nothing really helps because both teams are playing to their utmost. That was the case in the 1977 Stanley Cup playoffs when the Flyers and Boston Bruins engaged each other. Games went into overtime and rarely was there more than a one or two goal difference during any game. Yet the Flyers lost four in a row. This was a time of adversity but there was little that Clarke could do.

"We played well, they played well, particularly their goalie, Gerry Cheevers," Clarke recalls. "We had our shots but we just couldn't get any goals past him. So you must give the opposition credit, too. You can't get down on your teammates, start upbraiding them, yelling or doing other such ridiculous things. All you can do is give your best and if you are beaten by a team that is better at the time, you must accept the outcome. You don't have to like it—no one does—but there is little you can do."

One of Clarke's principal roles as the Flyers' captain is as a liaison between other players and Shero or between the players and management. Often a player will be unsure of his status with the team, so he goes to the player he feels most secure with—the captain. In this instance, Bobby will talk to Shero, if it involves something like playing time; or he'll go to the team's management if a player wonders whether or not he has enough security on the team to buy a home or invest his money in a local venture.

As for any advice about playing the game, Clarke will act only in a constructive manner. Perhaps he'll tell a player he is passing too much and not shooting enough, but Bobby feels that is something an interested player would do regardless of his position on the team. Still,

Shero says, there are times when Bobby will not hesitate one instant to speak up, either to straighten out a player who is slipping or even to get his own coach back into line.

"If there is a difference in opinion we settle it by acknowledging whoever is right and whoever is wrong," Shero says. "Sometimes I'll deliberately prepare a certain play and we'll work on it for a couple of hours. I know it's no good and Bobby's always the first one to seem to realize it. He'll say, 'That's enough of that nonsense.' And I tell the players, 'That's exactly what I want to hear.'

"Why? Because now we have everyone thinking. I don't want a group of trained dogs around me, doing only what they're told. I want them to do what is right. That's Bobby's great attribute. He insists that everything be right."

That is one point on which both agree.

"The practices actually mean more to a team than the games," Clarke maintains. "The games are overrated many times. But if you practice hard and the coach keeps your intensity at peak levels for the ninety minutes or so that you are working on the ice, then you'll have the same intensity during the game. I've always believed that you play as you practice. When it comes time for a game and a guy's not ready, there's nothing anyone can do to get him ready."

This philosophy has helped Shero and Clarke build a strong bond of mutual respect. Each will listen to the other and weigh each other's positions carefully. Shero does not agree with everything his captain may offer and will take time to point out where he feels Bobby is off the track. At the same time, if Shero feels a suggestion has some merit, he will try it, and if it works, fine; if it doesn't, Clarke and the other players know that Shero has tried to do something in their best interest.

Bobby sometimes makes suggestions to his coach during a game because he believes a player working on the ice gets a better feel for what is happening than the coach who stands behind the bench. Again, Shero may or may not follow the suggestion.

"Fred has two assistants working with him at every game, so he knows what is going on and he doesn't make too many mistakes," Clarke adds. "But if I think I can help by offering something, then he wants to hear it."

"I want to hear from him at all times," Shero says. "I lean heavily on Bobby because he can do things I can't do since he is a part of the team. A coach is not. He's like a father who depends on an older brother getting to a younger one because of their special relationship. Bobby or any good team captain can sense the pulse of a team better than any coach. He can feel when the mood of the players just isn't right. He can tell when we haven't been working hard enough and he can sense quickly when there's a rift developing in the ranks.

"The captain is more than a person for whom you just sew a 'C' on his sweater. In the professional ranks, they do much more than the average player. They are really like a coach but they've still got to produce according to their abilities. Coaches and management demand a lot from them and I think we should pay them more for the responsibilities they must assume."

Clarke does many things as a team captain which are not evident even to other players, Shero says.

"That is because he is the only athlete I've met, though I imagine there are others, who wants to do so much for the team that he'd do anything in his power to help a teammate even though it might hurt him as a player. Bobby never has won the scoring championship in the NHL, but I know he could have won it a couple of times if I had forced him to.

"We can be winning by five goals going into the last period and he won't go on the ice. Other stars love that situation because that's often the time when things come the easiest and they can pile up the points. We can be losing by four points, too, and he won't go on the ice. He'll say, 'Give those guys who haven't been getting much ice time some work. We might need them in the future and we'll keep them happy.'

"There are times when I'll come to him and ask, 'What can we do to pull so-and-so out of a slump? He's worried and not playing well because he's too tense.'

"He'll tell me, 'Don't worry. Break my line up and put him with me. I'll get him going. I'll sacrifice myself for him.' People who don't know what's going on will say, 'Hey, Clarke hasn't gotten any points tonight.' But they don't realize the job he is doing. He was pulling someone out of a slump, sacrificed his own line and himself.

"So glory means nothing to him. He wants to see

117

everybody do as well as they can. I haven't met too many athletes like that."

That doesn't happen only with Shero. A couple of years ago during the Stanley Cup playoffs, Rick Mac-Leish, one of the Flyers' top goal scorers, was having his problems. Clarke could see it and so could everyone else. Rather than allow it to become worse, Bobby made it a point to get with his teammate and to let him know that he thought he could do better.

"I simply told him that I didn't think he was playing up to his ability and that he had more ability than anyone else on this team," Clarke remembers. "I told him that if we were going to win, it would be because of players of his caliber giving a total effort, playing with every ounce of energy and determination they could muster. If you don't work hard, I said, then we're going to lose.

"That night he went out and scored two or three goals and we won, and then went on to win the Stanley Cup. Rick is like many players who are so talented. They don't always get the most from themselves because they are easygoing and everything they do comes so naturally to them they sometimes don't even realize they're not going all out.

"It's happened to me, too," Bobby adds. "Players have come to me and said, 'You're not doing such-and-such properly.' We talk about it and I'll make an adjustment. All of us need that at one time or other. It's not criticism in a negative sense, it is constructive. It is a great thing for a team when players pick each other up and try to help each other. Leadership is not strictly up to one person, everyone has to step in and help each other. We're all in this game together and we'll only be as good as all of us wish to be."

But Clarke acknowledges that a captain's job can be more effective with help from a core of veterans who feel strongly about a team's success and are willing to do something about it. He has lived with a group which came from nowhere to win two successive Stanley Cups. He remembers the times the players socialized together, building a spirit and camaraderie that spilled over onto the ice so that during a game everyone played because they were friends as well as teammates.

"After players are in one area for five or six years and are successful, it's only natural for them to drift in different directions," Clarke says. "They develop their own friends and instead of going out after practice or socializing after a game, they go their own way. Then, it's up to the captain and a few veterans to keep that togetherness feeling, particularly among the younger players who are coming on, and make them feel close to the team."

On the Flyers, players such as Van Impe, Gary Dornhoefer, Don Sileski, Bob Kelly, all with seven or eight years' experience, go out of their way to make the new players feel part of the club. They'll invite them to their homes for dinner or go out with them after practice. All of this, Clarke notes, "may seem like small potatoes but it is important for the overall good of the team."

"If you don't like the guys you're playing with," he adds, "you're not going to play that well."

The fact is that all of the Flyers have played well and

have been tremendously successful. But often with success comes complacency. Rarely has there been a successful team in professional sports which has not been struck with this dread disease, yet the Flyers so far have been immune. Clarke has played no small part in helping to maintain a high level of excellence and dedication. He is the first to acknowledge that winning brings success outside the ice rink in the form of endorsements, public appearances, and the like; it's tough to ask players to curb something that brings them extra money and greater public recognition, but occasionally outside activities interfere with a player's game.

"All professional athletes have a short career and we all understand that," he says. "You just can't demand that a player not make some extra money on the outside because that can be important to his future. But if you see a guy giving so much time off the ice to such things that it begins to affect his play, something must be done. The overall good of the team must come first or else none of us would be successful.

"I might talk to the player and try to help him realize that everything he is getting is because of his playing so well. I can't demand that he stop the outside activities but a smart player will realize that once his level of play begins to slip badly, he may be gone and then there are no more of those outside goodies. I think my job is to make the player aware of the situation. After that, what he does is up to him."

Players outside the Flyers also see Clarke's influence

in this area. Montreal's goalie, Ken Dryden, says that Bobby is the sole reason the Flyers haven't succumbed to deadening complacency after winning consecutive NHL titles.

"How can you lie back when the team leader is out there giving everything he has?" Dryden asks. "I can't think of anyone in any sport who has come close to him as a leader."

To which Fred Shero adds: "Amen."

PHOTOGRAPH BY UNITED PRESS INTERNATIONAL

YVAN COURNOYER

When the talk is about hockey, the name most often equated with excellence is the Montreal Canadiens. That is because of their image of unparalleled excellence and a history of what seems like one Stanley Cup championship after another in the National Hockey League. Hardly a year goes by when Les Habitants, as they are known in Montreal, are not favored to win the NHL title and most often—fifteen times during a thirty-one-year span following World War II—they did just that. Six other times they reached the Cup finals and lost, meaning that the Canadiens were involved in twenty-one of thirty-two Stanley Cup finals from 1946 to 1977.

That is an amazing record, one that cannot be matched by any other team in professional sports, and one that makes it easy to understand why the Canadiens are the best known and most respected hockey team in North America. There are solid reasons for this success, foremost being that their players always are among the best in the game. Right now, everyone knows Guy Lafleur, Jacques Lemaire, Ken Dryden, Larry Robinson, Serge Sevard, and Yvan Cournoyer . . . and before them and already in hockey's Hall of Fame, Maurice (The Rocket) Richard, Jean Beliveau, Bernie (Boom-Boom) Geoffrion, Dickie Moore, and Doug Harvey. Add the great leadership from fine coaches and excellent management and the results not only are a hatful of Stanley Cup championships but a great solidarity that seems to mean that the Canadiens almost are more than a hockey team.

Indeed, some think they are, with a tradition that has become as much a part of the team as the players on the ice. Playing against or even watching the Canadiens, means playing against or watching what has become a dynasty of total excellence. Everyone expects them to win and to excel, and rarely is that expectation ever disappointed. There is little doubt that the tradition affects opposing teams; the Canadien players declare steadfastly that it affects them and propels them toward playing their best in every game.

Against this backdrop, unique in all of competitive sports, it is difficult to imagine that such a team would need a captain—or, if it had one, that the captain would have much to do. But perhaps the key ingredient of the Canadiens' success over so many years is the great leadership from among their players. Their captains have included men like Rocket Richard, Beliveau, and Henri Richard, the Rocket's younger brother. These men believed in and carried on the great traditions that the team had created and insisted that every player follow their example.

It is no different in recent seasons when Yvan Cournoyer became the team's captain. He is the oldest of the current Canadiens but he also is the most respected. That great respect is one reason why his teammates, in a departure from the past, elected him to succeed Henri Richard when the Pocket Rocket retired a few seasons ago. In the team's method of operation, he is the one necessary link to past traditions, which are carried among the new group of Canadiens and which then will be passed on to the Montreal teams of the future.

Cournoyer has all the superb qualities of the great Montreal players. Like many who play for the Canadiens, he is a native of Quebec Province where the French-Canadian heritage has deep and abiding roots and is a point of great pride. For youngsters, hockey is the national pastime and that means dreams of someday playing for the Montreal Canadiens, as youngsters in the United States dream of playing baseball for the New York Yankees or football at Notre Dame.

And just as the Yankees were always expected to be baseball's champions and Notre Dame was expected to win every game, millions of Canadians expect Montreal to win against all opponents.

"In our city," says coach Scotty Bowman, "you're expected to win them *all*."

The players have the same expectations. They also have great individual talent and tremendous pride in what that talent has accomplished. This has always been a team of not one or two stars but often of nearly a dozen, many like Yvan, who wanted nothing more since their youth than to play hockey for the Canadiens and whose pride in their team and its heritage encouraged their fans to expect the team "to win them all."

It obviously takes a special kind of person to be captain of such a team. Yvan, since 1974, has been that man, leading his teammates because they respected him and because he has always been an all-out hockey player. Like many hockey players, he is not big by the standards we measure many athletes—five feet, seven inches and about 175 pounds. But in hockey, great size is not always a prerequisite to being a good player. When his teammates call him "The Roadrunner," you know exactly where his physical skills are strongest—flashing speed that hardly has diminished in the years since 1963 when he first joined the Canadiens. From his right wing position, this great speed often keys Montreal's offense and sets him whizzing past defensemen before they can recover, enabling him to swoop down upon opposing goaltenders who become almost frozen by this whirlwind attack.

Certainly Yvan does not do all this by himself, but he has played well enough over the years and has distinguished himself in his personal approach to the game to become the leader of this very talented hockey team. He has the maturity and the experience to build a rapport that bridges the great Canadien teams of the sixties and seventies. The players respect equally his judgments off the ice and his play on the ice, yet they know he is not the type of person who will flaunt his captaincy and turn from leader to boss, something that is very important to them.

Their captain, at no time, can be pushy or snippy; nor can he go around constantly giving advice or simply backslap. With so much talent and such a record of achievement, the Canadien players do not need unsolicited or unnecessary advice on how to play the game or pep talks on how to approach it. If anything, all they might ever need is the example of a man who never lets up, who realizes what the team's great heritage really means to its fans and management, and who is willing to speak for them any time the occasion arises, knowing that his voice will be heard and his views given serious consideration.

That is why they elected him their captain.

Cournoyer has seen this happen with Henri Richard and Beliveau and learned his lessons watching them. In fact, Beliveau was Cournoyer's roommate during his early years with the Canadiens and the two often talked about the responsibilities a Montreal captain had to assume. Jean's personality was different from Cournoyer's, though not by much; it was totally different from the fiery and intense Richard, whose leadership could be quite forceful.

"Being a captain, by itself, doesn't mean a thing on the Canadiens or in junior hockey unless the captain has great pride in his team, his teammates, and wants nothing more in this world than to win every game," Cournoyer says. "He must give a good example, for instance never being late for practice or a game. Jean and Henri used to talk about that. You could see the great pride and determination on their faces whenever they talked about the Canadiens and what the team meant to them. Being captain only meant they were able to give the example of all that they felt.

"Since I was closer to Jean Beliveau I knew how much he felt about his captaincy. He used to talk to me about how necessary it was for every player to give a total effort, for the team to play as one person. 'Sometimes,' he used to say, 'it is more necessary to do that when you are as successful as Montreal is than if your team is just striving to be successful. Everyone is looking to beat you and only by sticking together can you be successful.'

"I've been on a Stanley Cup winner eight times in my first fourteen years in the NHL and I totally believe that is necessary. Sometimes, even on the Canadiens, it is up to the captain to see that this spirit is sustained."

Cournoyer remembers the semifinal round of the 1971 Stanley Cup playoffs when Montreal trailed the Boston Bruins 3–1 in the best-of-seven series and was ready to play the next game at Boston Garden. Before the game, Beliveau addressed his fellow players in what could have been his last appearance before them as captain since he intended to retire when the playoffs ended.

"We can go two ways," Cournoyer remembers this great player telling his team. "People say there is no way we can come back and win. We can believe that and go out and let the Bruins beat us. Or we can go out and believe that this series is not over, that we still have a chance and we can beat the Bruins. No Montreal team ever has quit before and I don't want to be a member of the first one that ever does."

The Canadiens went out and not only beat the Bruins in that game but won the series 4–3 and went on to defeat the Chicago Black Hawks in seven games to win the Stanley Cup. Their play, everyone agreed, was absolutely inspired and a model for those who wonder about teamwork and total effort.

Rarely does any Montreal team captain ever have to give that kind of pep talk. If anything, the problem that accrues from so much success is keeping the team interested and competitively sharp. In the 1976–1977 season, for example, the Canadiens lost only eleven games; the year before, just fourteen, and in both seasons went on to win the Stanley Cup.

"Our biggest problem," Coach Bowman says, "is boredom. Our players are pretty good at motivating themselves but sometimes it's tough to keep them from getting bored with their division. This is where a player like Yvan is so beneficial. He doesn't have to say anything but when he goes out on the ice, he is all business.

"The other players see this and with the respect that he

has generated for himself plus that which goes with being captain, he lights a fire, if that is what it takes."

Again, a team with the great pride of the Canadiens is totally conditioned to know that every game will be a war because every opponent is geared especially to do its best against them. That is why Cournoyer or any other of the team's leaders rarely must give their teammates a little jab. In fact, every one of them seems to enjoy the challenges of playing one of the NHL's other good teams or of meeting a team that has been going exceptionally well over a period of time.

Cournoyer remembers an early season game in the 1976–1977 season against the New York Islanders at Nassau Coliseum on Long Island. The Islanders were riding a ten-game unbeaten streak, but that night Montreal soundly defeated them, 5–1.

"We knew going into the game that we had something to prove," he recalls. "We thought about the game for a long time and in our own way we talked about it among ourselves. We were determined we had to go out there, get ahead of them, and not let them get the jump.

"It happened later in the season against the Flyers. We had won four straight games against them in the Stanley Cup the previous year, and we knew they were never going to forget it. We played this particular game in the Montreal Forum and put fifty-five shots on Bernie Parent, the Flyers' goalie. We found out afterward that no one ever had that many shots on a Flyers' goalie, but we won, 6–4.

"That is the nature of this team. All of us are capable

of rising to any occasion and bringing out the best in each other. It has been that way with the Canadiens, with few exceptions, since I joined the team. Everyone seems to know what is expected of him and no one really has to go around and get guys up for a big game. What a player, including the captain, does on the ice is what is important and carries the most weight."

Don't think for a moment that Cournoyer's job as a player or a captain isn't necessary or appreciated. Bowman recalls being very concerned when the 1976–1977 season began because Yvan did not have a good training camp. He didn't score a goal in any of the preseason games and the team scored many.

"Yvan's biggest assets on the ice are his skating and shooting," Bowman says. "We didn't see that spark in the camp and it really bothered me. Yet by mid-season, before he was injured, he had scored thirteen goals and twenty-one assists and was skating as hard and fast as ever."

Above that, say his teammates, there is a definite need for his leadership. Dryden, the team's goaltender and one of its most articulate spokesmen, says even the Canadiens, with all of their talent and success, need someone they can turn to.

"If there wasn't a captain, there would be confusion," Dryden says. "We picked Yvan because of his great experience and ability to deal with every player on an equal level. There are players more talented than him but who don't have his experience. There are others nearly as experienced but who aren't any more talented. He brings each man into a proper focus and maintains a consistent relationship among everyone. He has the one key element a captain of the Canadiens must have—total respect, from everyone . . . the coach, the players, and management.

"A captain of a different sort, one who would be too vocal or too aggressive, would not be an appropriate person to lead this particular team," Dryden adds. "We have many very strong, very proud, and very talented individuals. If you had someone as captain who was particularly authoritative, aggressive, and demanding, there would be a very destructive type of reaction."

Cournoyer agrees, noting that his teammates made his captaincy easy from the beginning because of their trust in his judgment and their willingness to accept his leadership. They knew him and knew the type of person he was. One of the Canadiens noted that Henri Richard, his predecessor, was often very tart with the players, some of whom resented that attitude and really didn't need to be badgered too much.

"Henri was a very proud man," the player said, "and he took personally any game that we lost or didn't particularly play well. It bothered him and some of us felt he never made allowances that there will be times when we do not—perhaps cannot—play as well as we should. Remember, the Richard name goes back to the very heart of the Canadiens' rise to greatness and he may have felt anything that diminished that image was a slur against him."

Réjean Houle, Cournoyer's roommate and one of the team's new young stars, says there are other differences.

"Henri was from the old group of Canadiens and there wasn't a great deal of communication between player and player, or between coach and player," he notes. "I had a great deal of respect for him but it was difficult for younger players to get through to him. His strong influence was in a game because he worked so hard and didn't have to talk. He certainly was more emotional than Yvan, but all the Richard brothers were emotional and at certain times it came out."

That is an interesting comparison as to the correct type and time for leadership. Richard's fiery disposition and his great will for winning would probably be much more accepted among a group of younger players who had no record of success and were hungry to challenge the best teams. With a team like the Canadiens, there is the need to strike a compromise and realize that the values of each man are more necessary, though Richard never lost either the respect or the affection of his teammates.

It is no different with Cournoyer, though his different style probably is much more appreciated by the Canadiens. Some players say he accomplishes more with this group of players because of his quieter ways. The players' respect has grown during the time he has been captain because he wears the "C" on his sweater and does not dangle it over the head of each individual.

"He is very accessible," Houle noted. "You don't have

to have a hockey problem to approach him. He'll listen to anything you might want to tell him and if he can't help you work it out yourself, then he'll try and find a remedy, either with the coach or with someone else in the organization who might be able to help. He seems to realize that everyone plays better when their minds are clear. This and his willingness to boost a guy's confidence are his biggest contribution as our captain."

Houle could have added "any time, day or night" because Cournoyer has made himself totally available to every player, regardless of the hour. He recalls a player coming to his hotel room in Philadelphia at six-thirty one morning, concerned because he was not getting enough playing time, asking Yvan's help to try and remedy the situation.

"It was a small problem," he recalls. "But the important thing was that it bothered the man. I could see his concern and I also can see the necessity of keeping every player ready for a game in case he's needed. He might be the one who would get us a victory some night. After I talked with the player, I took the problem to Scotty and got him together with the player to try and work out the situation. That was all I could do but it was necessary for me to do that much."

Bowman sees Cournoyer's value in other areas as well. He acknowledges that the Canadiens have not invested their leadership in just one player and don't expect the responsibility to be limited to a single player. He appreciates a player who is outgoing in the locker room, citing former winger Jim Roberts as a good example.

"Some players do that kind of job on the ice, some in the locker room," Bowman says. "Both are important provided they do not overstep themselves. In Yvan's case, he is an inspirational type of leader on the ice and that is what we look for more than anything else in our captain. That he can do other things with the players is fine and also necessary. But our players are such that they are a very self-sufficient group who pretty much take care of themselves away from the ice. But every team needs a player who will show the way once the game begins."

There is a good, solid relationship, not only between Bowman and Cournoyer, but between the Canadien coach and all of his players. Still, the players take their lead from their captain. If Yvan sees that the team is not doing something that can improve its performance during a game, he'll tell his coach; or if he thinks that by changing the way the team is doing something it will help, he'll tell him also.

"If we are behind in a game, I also try to get everyone together so we can come back and win," he adds. "And if we're in front, we always try to keep the players' minds on their business so we don't lose the lead. The big thing is to maintain a level of sharp play and help the coach where possible. Scotty is good that way. We try to help him and he tries to help us. That's why we have been so successful the last few years.

"He knows too there is a core of six or seven veterans, including myself, whom he can count on, players like Serge Sevard, Larry Robinson, and Ken Dryden. Sometimes if a problem arises, we get together among ourselves and work it out. If that's not possible, then I'll take it to Scotty and work from there. But the important thing is that we never allow any problems, from guys not playing enough, or being late for practice or getting lousy seats for the playoffs, to bother us. Every player knows where he can come if there is a problem or I know where I can turn to help solve a problem."

Houle, who once played for the Quebec Nordiques in the World Hockey Association after being raised in the Canadiens farm system, has seen two different styles at work. As Cournoyer's roommate, he also has gotten a better view of his overall role with the team. He too cites Cournoyer's ability to keep the team together as the one big plus of his captaincy.

"Yvan shows by example what we should do because he always works harder than anyone else, in practice or in a game," Houle says. "He's always been with the Canadiens and he has the attitude that Montreal wants from one of its hockey players. He takes good care of himself and he is the type of player who hates to lose. This is the attitude he tries to pass on to the other players, but not in such a way that it turns them off.

"He carries this same style onto the ice. He is always cool and composed and doesn't do foolish things like draw unnecessary penalties. He's always in the game and plays as hard as possible. When the coach needs him he's always ready to do the job. Believe me, the young guys on the Canadiens follow his example."

All of which translates into one message:

Yvan Cournoyer is the perfect captain for what has almost become the perfect hockey team.

PHOTOGRAPH BY UNITED PRESS INTERNATIONAL

ROGER STAUBACH

The big scoreboard at Metropolitan Stadium told the entire story. The Dallas Cowboys trailed the Minnesota Vikings 14–10 with just 40 seconds to play in the game and had the ball at midfield. In those circumstances the Cowboys didn't seem to have any chance to win because they had to score a touchdown against one of the National Football League's best defenses. Under any conditions such a feat was almost impossible so there were very few watching in the chill of the Viking stadium or in front of television sets across the country who gave Dallas any chance at all.

In the Cowboy huddle, Roger Staubach held no such thoughts. Giving up . . . conceding defeat, regardless of how inevitable it seemed, was not in his nature. As he looked at the faces of the ten other players he could see as they looked back at him, it was not their style either . . . at least, not just yet. Perhaps deep down in their hearts they were ready to concede but when their quarterback broke the huddle and sent them to the line of scrimmage, they still believed victory was possible.

Certainly, Drew Pearson, the Cowboys' swift wide receiver, believed. Pearson thought about only one thing as his legs carried him faster and faster toward Minnesota's end zone: "The ball . . . I've got to catch the ball."

And as he moved, Staubach watched for just a couple of seconds because that was all the time he had. Directly in front of him, desperate Minnesota linemen huffed and puffed to get him, pawing with huge arms and hands, hoping to pin his arms or throw him to the ground . . . anything to prevent him from throwing the football.

Before the ball was ever snapped, before the game was ever played, they knew about Roger Staubach. They knew that he had the unique knack of somehow producing miracles in a football game. Only three years before, he had entered a playoff game in San Francisco with just minutes to play and the Cowboys behind by two touchdowns. Somehow, some way, he threw two touchdown passes against the 49ers that enabled a Cowboy team everyone thought was beaten to win another amazing football game.

Since his sophomore year at the Naval Academy he had been performing such feats, coming up with exciting plays and tingling finishes. Everyone, from the President of the United States to the ordinary paying spectator, had watched him perform under countless similar pressure situations. And they marveled at this ability.

So it was on this frosty December Sunday in Minnesota when Roger Staubach could wait no longer to throw the football. It came out of his hand as his arm swung in a naturally graceful arc and flew downfield without a flutter, true and on such perfect course that it appeared hurled by a computer-fed missile launcher. As it began its downward course, two men, one clad in a purple jersey, another in white, converged and jostled each other, desperately trying to catch it.

Amazingly . . . one did catch it. It was Drew Pearson, his white jersey with the vivid blue No. 88, clutching the ball between his arm and hip, skipping around defensive back Nate Wright and into the end zone for the winning touchdown.

On the clock: only 32 seconds remained to be played. Roger Staubach had done it again, just as he once did before 100,000 screaming people at the University of Michigan; before the same number in the vastness of Philadelphia's John F. Kennedy Stadium; and before a sun-drenched crowd in the New Orleans Sugar Bowl when a Super Bowl title was on the line. This, as one admiring opposing coach once said, was no ordinary young man.

It was no wonder that the Dallas Cowboys elected him as one of their captains after just a few seasons in the NFL and that coach Tom Landry, on his own, later

141

made the appointment permanent. A captain, Landry always maintained, must know how to win and be capable of proving it to his teammates under all imaginable conditions and circumstances.

Staubach certainly has accomplished that during his football career. He was only a sophomore at the Naval Academy in 1962 when he stepped into the bright, warm, autumn sunshine in Philadelphia and dazzled an Army team that was touted to be far superior. John F. Kennedy, the President of the United States, watched that day and later remarked that he had never seen one player cause so much to happen. It was not the old Navy man in Kennedy who was speaking. The remark was made in admiration of what he had witnessed.

One year later, just a few days after President Kennedy was assassinated, Roger Staubach was named winner of the Heisman Trophy, though only a junior, and was the most talked about college football player in the nation. So great were the pressures and the adulation that his coach at the Naval Academy, Wayne Hardin, decided being captain of the football team would be too much. Though Fred Marlin was elected, there are many who still feel that Staubach could have done the job and, though he never tried or even thought about upstaging Marlin's role, was in fact the source of the team's leadership.

Staubach was also an excellent baseball player and later in his senior year was named captain of Navy's team. As in football, his regard for his team was utmost.

Being captain meant providing whatever was required to help the team be successful. When the Middies played the University of Maryland Roger was sidelined with a pulled hamstring muscle in his leg. Coming into the bottom of the ninth inning, Navy trailed by two runs but loaded the bases. Though he knew that anything hit on the ground would be useless because he couldn't run, Staubach asked to pinch hit. And seconds later, the ball slammed off his bat and hit the left field wall. Three runs crossed the plate and Roger hobbled into second base with a game-winning double.

"The intensity that he showed when something positive had to be accomplished was unforgettable," L. Budd Thalman, then the sports information director at the Naval Academy and one of Roger's early supporters, notes today. "He'd step out front and do the job. It was no big thing for him and he didn't expect others to make something from it. It was as much a part of his nature as the great skills he produced in athletic competition."

Of course, those are the qualities that every good and effective captain must possess. Staubach, like Bob Johnson of the Cincinnati Bengals, has been a team captain at every major level of competition. Like Johnson, he was even captain of the College All-Star football team. In football, he has often equated his early captaincies with being a team's quarterback, but others disagree.

"You'd have to have been a blind man not to see that he deserved the honor," Otto Graham, who coached Staubach's College All-Star team in 1965, notes.

With the Cowboys, it has been the same way. After Tom Landry began rebuilding his championship teams in the mid-seventies, he placed great trust in the work of his captains. Once taciturn and not always too concerned with what or how his players felt, Landry instituted weekly meetings with his captains, sounding them out on problems, asking them to handle certain duties better left between player and player, all designed to keep open the lines of communication so necessary for team success.

Staubach recalls a team meeting where Landry noted the frequency of injury was often determined by a player's ability and willingness to stay in shape. Dallas has a prescribed regimen for every player and expects it to be followed. But one of the players, injured at the time, took his coach's comment as an implication that he had somehow not followed the training rules. The next day, he told Roger he didn't think it proper that he was singled out for criticism, though Landry had mentioned no one by name.

"All the players knew who was hurt and not playing so I said, 'Coach Landry, it really bothered the players that you made it sound like it was one player's fault that he got injured,'" Staubach recalls. "He said, 'Oh no, that wasn't meant to be a personal criticism at all. I just wanted to alert everyone to keep working to prevent injuries.' That day at the team meeting he clarified what he meant. Afterward there wasn't a player who had hurt feelings or felt he was being picked on.

"It was important to the team and to coach Landry

that he know about those feelings. At the same time, I'll get complaints from players during training camp about curfews or food or living conditions which may, or may not, be important. I won't carry every little complaint because it will undermine his judgment in my ability to see what is important and what is not. He knows I don't bring a problem to his attention unless it is for the specific good of one player or the overall team, and will prevent any serious problems from arising."

To Staubach, this is the heart and soul of his captaincy. He is not afraid to stand up to a player and say, "I don't think that's important enough to take to the head coach." At the same time, if he does take a problem into Landry's office, he also will stand up and, if necessary, stick by his judgment as to the seriousness of a particular situation.

Like Bob Johnson of the Bengals, and George Kunz of Baltimore, he also feels the responsibility as a captain for seeing to it that the players keep working in practice and that each man gives as much help and cooperation so that the team will benefit. Sometimes he will meet with the other captains and talk over particular problems. Often after a bad game, he and the Cowboy captains will meet with the players and try to talk out the nitty little problems that might be detracting from a full effort.

"Even on professional teams, and good teams like the Cowboys, players look constantly for leadership," Staubach says emphatically. "As good athletes, they are able to go out and do their job naturally. But when things go wrong or get a bit tough, natural athletic ability isn't always enough. Any person, whether a professional athlete or not, can become unsure at those times and need someone to help pick him up.

"For a captain to try and do that, he should be playing as well as possible. If he isn't, it is hard to go to someone else and tell him what to do. In my own case, as a quarterback I'm always involved, so I can approach a player having a problem and try to help him work it out. This puts me in a unique position. I'm older, I work very hard at my job and have the respect of the players. They know I'm giving everything that I've got and they appreciate it. That is a very important thing.

"I don't try to be one of the boys. We have a young team and I'm older. We have five children at home so I don't have the opportunity to go out and do things off the field with many of the players. I know there are other captains in the NFL who can do this and there are other quarterbacks who have made it a point of buddying around with their teammates.

"Bobby Layne, who was finishing his career when I was at the Naval Academy, was a quarterback like that. I don't have his personality but I always respected him for his competitiveness and his freewheeling manner. In his own style, he was a great leader. I'm competitive too but my style is a bit quieter. Still, I believe I'm just as effective."

Regardless of style, Staubach maintains that there always is a need for a team captain to be willing to help

146

teammates in times of duress. Never has he found a player, in college or in professional football, who didn't appreciate some kind of help because all they really are looking for is an answer to what might be wrong with their game. They aren't asking a captain or any of the team's other leaders to do their jobs for them; just to offer something that might help them do their own job better.

To Staubach, this is the true meaning of leadership, which he defines simply as "the ability to have other people follow you." There are no set methods for this to happen. Every person is different not only in how he leads but in his response to leadership. Roger is not of the rah-rah school but before a game, he tries to talk to each player in the locker room. Sometimes it is just a quiet word of encouragement; sometimes it will be a word or two about a play or some strategy; often it is nothing more than a handclasp or a pat on the back.

On the field his total concentration is on the game itself. He rarely thinks about taking time to encourage a player or to try and fire up his team if things are not going well. He sees Bert Jones, the Baltimore Colts' excellent quarterback, as typical of the leader who always is fired up, urging on his teammates. That's not Roger's style, nor is it really the Cowboys' style, which is patterned after Landry's cool, calm approach to football where thorough preparation and execution are the keys to winning.

"The key to leadership is how you get things done,"

Staubach says simply. "Next is your own particular charisma in doing something and then the respect your teammates have for what you accomplish. A quarterback, by the very nature of his position on the team, is a natural leader because he is involved in everything that happens with the offense. That is his primary responsibility and if there are moments when the team needs some vocal leadership, there are others with less to think about who can provide it. No one has a lock on that area and no one ever should be content to sit back and wait for someone else to do it."

"Roger Staubach has true leadership," says Tex Schramm, the team's president. "The other players see it and respect it. It's just there—self-assurance, confidence, maturity—whatever it is that defines leadership. He's not a holler guy. He just sets an example that others understand. There are a lot of quarterbacks but the great ones are those who have that leadership ability. Roger makes people believe."

Another Cowboy executive noted that Staubach actually seems to "seek the pressure of leadership. He really believes that the team on the field is his responsibility, that its success or failure is a direct reflection on himself. He is willing to pay the price of leadership, too, partly due to his military training in that he understands the leader must be isolated, must be willing to stand alone or go out front to accomplish what he believes to be necessary."

Coach Landry is another whose admiration for his

quarterback is almost boundless. It began when Staubach was determined to fulfill his four-year commitment to the Navy after graduation from Annapolis but yet continued, in his free time, to acquaint himself as soundly as possible with the Cowboys' intricate offensive system.

"You rate your great star players on dedication and intensity," Landry says, with the tacit understanding that all other requirements of talent are there. "When you look back at the dedication and the sacrifice Roger was willing to undergo in order to become a professional football player—why it's unbelievable. He gave up his leave time, he studied films and playbooks, he came to our training camps when he still was a naval officer. He did everything we asked of him. His great consistency is that he still is doing it."

Landry so believed in Staubach that he was willing to risk important games. After Roger bailed out the Cowboys in that hair-raising 1972 playoff victory over the 49ers, Landry named him as the starting quarterback in the NFC title game against Washington the following week. Many felt then, and still do, that Landry made the wrong decision because injuries kept Roger from playing most of that season while Craig Morton had played and played well. It was Morton whom Staubach had relieved in the 49er game. The Cowboys were seemingly heading for defeat and Landry felt so buoyed by Roger's great penchant for getting victory where defeat seemed inevitable that he cast aside all logical reasons for not making him the starting quarterback. The year before Staubach had led the Cowboys to a victory in the Super Bowl and was named the game's most valuable player.

The Cowboys and Staubach lost to Washington in that NFC playoff game but the following season, and for every season thereafter, Staubach was back as Landry's starting quarterback. For the first time since the team was founded in 1960, meaning through the terms of Eddie LeBaron, Don Meredith, and Morton, Landry had the leader he knew his team needed to be successful and he never has wavered in his trust.

It was that way at the Naval Academy too, according to Wayne Hardin, who was the Middies' coach during the seasons that Staubach played for Navy.

"He was a leader by example," Hardin recalls. "You could almost see the electricity move from one person to another when he was around. I've never been around a football player, before or since, who could do that for a team. I remember that at the end of his senior year, nearly every member of that team had him autograph a picture. One of them told me later, 'Coach, everyone has a hero and Roger will always be mine.'"

Mike Ditka, who played with Roger on the Cowboys NFL championship team in 1971 and later became a coach at Dallas, claims that if you tell Staubach he can't do something "he'll go right out and prove you wrong. That's because he is such a great leader. He just doesn't quit. And he does his leading by showing and not by talking. It is so important for a team to have that solid leadership base to head off the inevitable problems which always arise during six months or so when everyone is together all the time."

Of course, Staubach has help from the other Cowboy captains. Add to them the core of solid, veteran players who form a natural leadership group and the team is well supported. That support still is under Coach Landry's control. He has very definite beliefs about what makes a team strong so he exercises a good measure of influence over what the players can and cannot do. This is not bad, Staubach says quite strongly, because he has taken into account what his players feel they must do and what he knows they can do and still be successful.

"He's really listened to us," Roger adds. "He's tried to meet with the players and take their needs into account. But when the final word comes down, it is his word that counts and that is all there is to it. We know that and we accept it. Besides, it's hard to argue or to oppose a system that has been so successful."

A winning record hasn't always been a deterrent to player opposition on other teams. Even Paul Brown, who like Landry is one of the greatest coaches in professional football history, was once fired because players success-fully opposed his methods of doing things and—mis-takenly, as it turned out—convinced the team's president that they were correct and their coach was wrong. Those instances are rare and generally are avoided by the posi-tive leaders on a team stepping forward and doing what they know to be correct.

Staubach has experienced such problems during his

years with the Cowboys. During a strike of NFL players prior to the opening of training camp a few seasons back, Roger refused to go along with the union's decision to boycott and reported to the team's site in California. The union's executive director, furious over the decision, made a slurring remark about Roger that also reflected on anyone else who ever had served in the Navy.

"I'd hate to have been at Pearl Harbor with him," the man said.

Staubach and some of his teammates were furious, but for different reasons. To Roger, the remark was an insult to anyone who has served the Navy in time of war, particularly to those men who were at Pearl Harbor when it was attacked without warning by the Japanese in December, 1941.

To his teammates, the remark was tasteless and totally unnecessary. Though many of them chose to honor the Player Association's decision to boycott training camp, they respected Roger's decision to disagree, none seeing it as a selfish or self-centered move. Bob Lilly, then in his final season with the Cowboys and perhaps the greatest defensive tackle in NFL history, told everyone, "The more conscientious you are, the harder this thing is on you. I guarantee you that Roger does not lack for guts or courage and anybody who knows him knows that to be absolutely true."

Staubach remembers thinking a long time about that situation before coming to training camp. He studied the issues, talked to his teammates and to the union's executive director. He finally realized that regardless of his decision, there was no easy way out.

"It made a lot more sense to me if a person stood up and did what he believed right rather than to go along with a position that really had little common sense behind it," he says. "This had nothing to do with me being a team captain. It was a matter of what I felt was right and wrong, and I had to do what I thought was right, regardless of how some of the other players felt. I respected their decision to stay out of camp and they respected mine to report. Nothing ever was said once we all got together and that is how it should be with any group."

Staubach always has been a stand-up guy. A couple of years ago he got into a fist fight in training camp with another Cowboy quarterback over a personal slur that was hurled at Drew Pearson. Pearson, besides being a co-captain, is also one of Roger's close friends, and Staubach instantly criticized the other quarterback for making the remark. When the slurs continued, Roger invited the man to step to the sidelines and settle the matter with fists.

"I don't advocate fighting to settle an issue," Roger is careful to stress. "But on this occasion, I felt a man's honor and reputation were being mocked. That's not right. He also was my friend and teammate and for another teammate to ridicule him also was not right. So I just couldn't stand out there and listen to him being torn down and not do anything about it. I asked the other guy to cut it out but that didn't do any good. Then I got mad and felt the only way to put a stop to it was to challenge the guy directly. He was in a position where he either had to prove himself right by answering the challenge or to prove how wrong he had been by backing down."

Roger won his point, the fight, and the admiration of his teammates. Two days later, the player stormed out of camp after trying to start another fight and never again played for the Cowboys. But the important effect was that Staubach would not compromise his own beliefs or his strength of will to appease another player. That was the very basis of his upbringing in Cincinnati, Ohio, and during his years in Purcell High School, New Mexico Military Institute, and at the Naval Academy where as a naturally gifted athlete, he always excelled. That meant he always was in the spotlight, beginning with his years as a Little League player. It is not unnatural for any young person to begin to feel like a "big deal" with the focus of such attention, but it wasn't that way in his home.

"Being a hero seemed like such a big deal," he recalls, "but my parents kept telling me I was just on one plateau and that if I thought I was so great, I wasn't going to achieve another level. I always had the desire to be the best and my parents accepted my interest in sports. They never pushed me but they always encouraged me. I guess I wanted to achieve for them.

"When I went to the Naval Academy, I learned things that will make me a success for the rest of my life. My

154

football career was in jeopardy any time I went into a game because a knee injury could have ended it forever. But the things I took away from Annapolis will never be lost. Football has been a very enjoyable and profitable existence but I always knew there were more important things. This is what I try and get across to our young players whenever we talk and to youth groups when I have public speaking engagements.

"I know a lot of young boys, especially those around junior high school age, are impressionable and like to emulate athletes. I only hope I can do my part in talking about the values of life and letting them know the great things we have in our country."

He carries over these principles to his athletic life without wearing them like a badge of honor. He does not flaunt either his fame or his deep-seated beliefs, yet will make no effort to conceal what he really believes if asked. His concerns about his personal life and his approach to football are closely associated with what he believes to be the correct way to live.

What this adds up to is an inner confidence, "a sense of security," he calls it, that comes from his knowing he has the ability to do something and do it successfully. It is what got him through those last-second victories against the 49ers and Vikings and that helped him instill the confidence in his teammates that they too could be successful.

"A professional athlete must have confidence and a desire to win," he says. "When you are a pro there's no

155

other reason for being out there. The idea, the emphasis, must be on winning. That's why I enjoy pressure situations. But I am a poor loser in the sense that I'll not accept failure. There probably is no shame in failing if you've done your best, but still I don't think anyone ever should be satisfied with not being successful.

"I remember my first two seasons with the Cowboys when I sat on the bench. I knew I could do the job. That bothered me the most. I began to worry that I would be typed as a player who was always talking about how good he could be but not that he was. Coaches hear that all the time from players who aren't playing regularly. Finally, I went to coach Landry and told him that if I couldn't play regularly for the Cowboys then I wanted to be traded elsewhere."

That is the true essence of not giving up, not settling for second best or just being satisfied—in the case of a professional athlete, just to collect a salary. Staubach says this same attitude should apply to every level of competition, that a person who knows he can play well never should be satisfied with anything but playing well.

It is the same in the overall approach—regardless of the level of competition—of being a team captain. He lists three major considerations that anyone can follow:

"The first is to work and try harder than the next person," he says. "Never fall short of what you're supposed to do and expect someone else to pick up the slack. Next, a captain never should expect anything more from the other players than he is putting forth himself. The captain must set the example as far as hard work and conditioning are concerned, and be willing to go along with the coach's rules and not complain.

"A captain also should be low-key when it comes to making criticisms about other team members. He can't go around hurting people's feelings, or being too pushy, or feeling he must reprimand a player every time a mistake is made. A captain can get his point across without being pushy. The thing to remember is that not everyone appreciates criticism and the worst thing a captain could do would be to turn off one of his players."

Not bad advice from someone who practices what he believes and has proven it is successful.

PHOTOGRAPH BY FOCUS ON SPORTS

JOHN HAVLICEK

With more than a dozen world championship banners hanging from the rafters of Boston Garden, you'd get the idea that the Boston Celtics play only for the glory of winning. Wrong! They play for pride—CELTICS PRIDE is what thousands upon thousands of New England bumper stickers proclaim. That is a key part of the heritage that has made them one of the greatest franchises in professional sports history.

They couldn't have had a better leader over the past decade than John Havlicek, perhaps the most amazing physical specimen ever to play professional basketball and one of the greatest ever to play any professional sport. Still going strong after sixteen seasons in the National Basketball Association, he lends truth to Bill Rus-

159

sell's view that he really isn't a flesh and blood human being but a bionic man!

John's great physical durability is well known. He has run thousands of miles up and down basketball courts never seeming to tire, playing forty and forty-five minutes, game after game, even past his thirty-fifth birthday. But more than his physical prowess is his mental approach to the game. Seemingly imperturbable, he relishes the last-second shot, the key pass or the clutch steal . . . anything that reeks of pressure. Rarely changing his expression, he plays the same way whether his team is thirty points ahead with a minute to play or one point down with seconds left . . . all-out!

In every sense of the word, he is the perfect team captain because no one ever has to wonder how he approaches any game. All they need do is follow his example.

That is one of the keys to the Celtics' continuing success. Following Havlicek's example means following an example set even before he came to Boston in 1962, when the Celtics were in the midst of winning eight consecutive NBA championships. Red Auerbach established a foundation of total dedication to winning and excellence—a Celtic tradition—when he coached the team and had Bob Cousy, Bill Russell, and Frank Ramsey as his captains before Havlicek.

The success of this team and those who play on it, including Havlicek, is very much tied in to what the players seriously refer to as "Celtics tradition." Havlicek agrees with present and former players who say that playing for the Celtics is as much playing basketball as it is assuming that tradition. That was how he viewed it when he joined the team and notes that every other successful player in Boston did the same thing. Walking into the Celtics offices or into Boston Garden with those championship banners hanging down, you know it is impossible to escape the feeling of this tradition. Consequently, no one wants to be the first to ignore the excellence and dedication demanded by such accomplishments and break that chain.

"I've tried to do the things I was taught and hope the other people following me will carry on this sense of tradition," Havlicek notes. "Dave Cowens and Jo-Jo White know what it's all about, and when I leave they'll pass it to others like Tom Boswell, Curtis Rowe, and Sidney Wicks, as well as the young players who come along."

It is easy to see the benefits to any team captain knowing that his players are striving as hard as he to continue this style of play. With everyone trying to do his best, his job becomes one of leadership by example. That's how it was when John joined the team with Cousy as captain, where the foundation was laid for his own outstanding captaincy.

"I thought that Cousy was the type of person who led with emotion, something I am not," Havlicek notes. "He was an individual who really could get a team moving from the style he played. He could make a couple of real crisp passes or real fancy moves and that seemed to increase the tempo and get everyone going."

Tom Heinsohn, once the Celtics coach, who played with Cousy and the other great Celtics players, sees a common thread running through everyone who ever had the captain's job: each led by example on the floor.

"Our captain didn't have to be out there grouching at everyone," Heinsohn adds. "It's more by his attitude toward his own game and the game in general than standing there being another coach on the floor. That's not what we looked for—another critic. We wanted a helpmate, someone who was more interested in helping than in criticizing. It's a very delicate line sometimes but it can be done. Most of the time the guy who does it in the least vocal way will have the greatest direct bearing because he will be out there playing hard, playing his game and working for the Boston Celtics."

That is John Havlicek, to a T. He's not a quiet man by any stretch of the imagination, but when he says something it has that much more impact because everyone knows it must be important. This is how he has grown into his job after having been appointed by Bill Russell in 1967 when Russ was the team's playing coach and near the end of his great career.

At the time, John was one of the team's youngest players and Russell was not only the coach but the Celtics' acknowledged leader, perhaps the game's most dominant player. Havlicek still was the team's "sixth man," where he would come into a game when the team needed a lift and go all-out for a specified period. Game after game, from the time that Ramsey did that job, teams found themselves suddenly being blown away with this quick burst of energy and talent coming off the bench.

When he wasn't playing, though, Havlicek was very much into the game. Long before the pre-game warmup, he painstakingly studied every opponent and built up a scouting report that he could use to his own advantage. Russell knew this. Bill knew too, from his first season as head coach, that he could not keep track of the myriad details and still concentrate on playing. By making Havlicek his captain, he gave John the responsibility of observing many things in the game and relied on him to bring them to his attention during a time-out. This was equivalent to being an assistant coach and a bit over-whelming, even for Havlicek.

"I'll do the best job I can," he told Russell.

"I know you will," Russell replied. "That's why I'm not going to tell you anything because I know you well enough to be sure of what you will do for us."

It was that way from the very first day that Havlicek joined the team after being cut by the Cleveland Browns of the National Football League. That he could compete in professional football, after not having played the sport since high school where he was a quarterback, showed the measure of his great athletic skills. With the Browns, he was tried as a wide receiver, where his lack of blazing foot speed caused Paul Brown reluctantly to let him go.

With the Celtics, he was expected to add the great

163

dimension of defense that had been his forte at Ohio State. But his constant movement without the ball seemed always to bring him open for a shot.

"So shoot," Auerbach told him. He did and worked to improve his offense with countless hours of shooting during the off-season. That demonstrated his unselfishness and his determination to be the best possible player. A defensive man, by nature, must be unselfish because he sacrifices the glory of point-making to perform what some feel is a thankless task.

Havlicek never has felt that way nor does he worry about who gets the points and who gets the glory. It is who gets the victories that counts most with him.

"I knew from the first time I played this game that the toughest guy to score on was the guy who kept after me all the time, nose-to-nose, basket-to-basket," he says. "The opposite also is true. The toughest guy to defend against is the guy who keeps running, who never lets up, never allows you to relax. I never worried about the physical part, about how much toll all that running would do to me. I read once where a doctor said you'd pass out before you did any real damage and I never passed out."

His unselfishness was also reflected in his willingness to become the Celtics' "sixth man" during his early seasons. Many think this a put-down because it suggests the player isn't good enough to be a starter. Nothing was further from the truth where Auerbach and the Celtics were concerned.

164

"John never was a sixth man with us," Auerbach declares. "People got the idea because I broke him in as a rookie the same way I did with Frank Ramsey. But Havlicek was never our sixth best player. He was always more like our third or fourth best player at that time and, remember, we were so deep in talent. But with John, I could afford the luxury of keeping him on the bench at the start of a game until I saw somebody on the other team dogging it or until we needed someone to get us running. Then I'd send him in."

Even in the past couple of years, Havlicek occasionally has gone back to that role, not because his talent has slipped but because "Tommy didn't have any positive influence coming off the bench. So he asked me to do it. Once you ascribe some type of notoriety for that position, as the Celtics have done, it's not a come-down to be asked to fill that role."

That is a perfect example of Havlicek's willingness to lead by example: never to be so caught up with his own importance or position on the team—he was the team captain at the time—that he felt a job was beneath his dignity. That, Russell recalls, was the precise reason why he had no qualms in appointing him team captain.

Because of Russell's great dominance, there was no way that Havlicek could overshadow him as a leader. So he didn't even try. But if any of the Celtics at that time, or later, ever wondered what their captain did, or even why he was appointed to the position, all they had to do was to watch him play, or study his approach to the game . . . run, run, run . . . move, move, move. It was the way he played in high school, at Ohio State, and why he made such an ideal "sixth man" with the Celtics.

"If you're going to play with me, you're going to have to play at my pace," he says. "I remember the seventh game of the 1969 playoffs against the Lakers. We were ahead at halftime by a substantial margin and I told Russell that the only way we can possibly lose the game is by slowing up. Russ and Sam Jones both were tired at that point so I told them, 'When we get the ball, give it to me and I'll push it up the floor as quickly and as hard as I can. Doing that should make everyone else play a little harder and a little faster because this is how we established our lead in the first half and we don't want to relinquish it.' Fortunately we held on to win by just two points but I think I had a significant effect in that victory by trying to set the pace."

Heinsohn, himself a captain at Holy Cross during his collegiate days and once Havlicek's roommate with the Celtics, feels this is the only style in which any captain can be effective. There are responsibilities which people have a right to expect a captain to live up to, regardless of his situation on the team.

"Most are in the example category," Heinsohn says. "It's a people thing. Anyone in a position of responsibility is responsible to people, not to things. If it were to things he'd be the manager of the ball club, picking up towels. But a captain's efforts should be toward helping people. In one instance it is the coach; in the other, the players."

Havlicek certainly knew this. He had been captain of every team he played on during his senior year in high school, and capped a great college career by being named captain of Ohio State's Big Ten champions. In fact, he got the vote of every Ohio State player except one—his own, and he voted for Jerry Lucas, the Buckeyes' all-American center.

"In high school," he says, "a captain usually is the player who produces the most because he is the one most likely to be looked up to. He's more or less been an example that has brought success and everyone wants to follow a successful person. In college, I was very surprised to be named captain. There were many players on our team who I felt could qualify. The reason I think I was selected was that I had a certain willingness and a diligence for work."

Diligence for work? While everyone knows the quick way to public recognition in basketball is to score gobs of points, Havlicek took a different tack. He became the team's best defensive player and in every game had the job of playing against the opposition's top scorer. He became so good, some of his teammates say, he'd complain if he thought he wasn't guarding the other team's number one man. Game after game, he'd hold 25-point scorers to 10 or 12, many of them all-Americans and later stars in the NBA.

"Even in practice," John recalls, "I'd be just as tough on my own teammates. I think this enabled the whole team to become better because they were being led by an example the coach really was trying to emphasize. There were never any other problems that would require meetings and such because all of us had been together for four years at Ohio State.

"So there really wasn't much for me to do other than lead by example and have a willingness to set the tempo and pace in practice. And if someone really didn't feel like going all-out, I'd say, 'Hey, you're really messing up practice. Why don't you take a blow and we'll get someone in here who really wants to work at it.' "

Those are the instances when Havlicek veers away from his quiet man demeanor and lays out in no uncertain terms how he feels about the way a player is performing. It doesn't happen very often but when he decides something needs to be said, he won't hesitate one instant to get someone—everyone, if he believes the team is at fault—straightened away.

There was a case late in a game a few years ago when the Celtics called a time out to set up two out-of-bounds plays. On the first one, the in-bounds pass was thrown to the wrong man. On the second, the center lined up wrong.

"I couldn't believe it," Havlicek recalls. "I doubt I'd ever done it before but I came back to the bench screaming and I had more to say in the locker room after the game. I told someone after the game I'd never been associated with such a dumb team. I said we had seven simple plays and if a guy comes into the league making $20,000 or $30,000 and can't learn seven simple plays, then he didn't deserve to be paid.

"The funny thing," John added, "was that we won that game. But it didn't make any difference to me. Winning doesn't excuse everything, particularly someone not being prepared or giving his best."

There also have been times, particularly when new players join the Celtics and begin to complain about some long-established principles of operation, that Havlicek has not hesitated to straighten out matters.

"It isn't your place to argue about certain things," he tells them. "If anyone is going to argue, then let the coach take it up. As for players bickering with each other, there is no place for it on this team.

"That is one of the things I'll jump on right away," he adds. "Other than that, I really don't find too many things to really talk about other than the fact that if we are going bad, the captain or one of the veteran players will call a team meeting and discuss what we are doing wrong. At that point, everyone becomes involved and the captain acts as mediator."

Still, Havlicek maintains close contact with all the Celtics players, during good times and not-so-good times. On rare occasions he has gone to players who may be having problems with shooting, or passing, or other technical points, though a coach normally is the first person to pick up such failings and will act immediately.

When he does try and help the player, he does it with a full range of experience to know exactly what the player is going through. Sometimes, all a player needs is some reassurance from the coach that he will continue to play because he may be the best player at that position and needs only to work his way out of the slump.

"I've gone through slumps and the only way you're going to get out of them is by playing your way out of them," Havlicek says. "I'll tell a player, 'The best thing you can have in a case like that is a sense of discipline to know when you're pressing and not pressing, when you're taking bad shots, and if you're doing that, then you're not going to help yourself.' "

Prior to the 1977 season, Havlicek sat down with Kevin Stacom, who was ready to begin his fourth year with the Celtics yet never had established a level of consistency. He had shown flashes of promise and from time to time had made some significant contributions. What Havlicek hoped to impress on him was that he needed to perfect his overall game so that no matter when he was called on to play, or under what conditions, he would be productive.

"Kevin," he said, "you've been here three years and you continue to make one mistake. You must improve your judgment. There are certain times when you play real well and then you'll turn around and diminish what you've done by making the same mistake you've made for three years. You're a great shooter but you pass up effective fifteen-foot jump shots and try to drive toward the basket against Artis Gilmore or Kareem Jabbar or the other big men and your shots are rejected.

"If you would just take that fifteen-foot jumper you'll be much better. Just think about that one shot because no one ever is going to tell you not to take it with your shooting talent. I've done things like that and this is something a person must learn when he comes to the Celtics. It's never been a matter of a person overshooting. No one's ever been criticized for that. It's a matter of taking bad shots that will draw criticism. If you get a hundred shots a game and they're good shots, no one is going to crab about it."

Most of the time, though, Havlicek exerts his strongest influence on the court, during a game. That is where he feels leadership is most effective because that is the time when other players recognize and respond to it most naturally. This has been particularly true in playoff games or in close games. The Celtics have built their strength around players with strong personalities or who simply won't quit. There are still thousands of broken hearts in Los Angeles, New York, Philadelphia, Phoenix, Milwaukee, and other NBA cities where the Celtics have beaten better teams during their astounding string of NBA titles.

"When the Celtics won a lot of championships in the sixties, there were teams who claimed they had better talent or were equal in talent. But I don't think they had the moral fiber from the first man to the tenth man that we had," Havlicek notes. "That is why it is important to have a nucleus of leaders on a team, not just one man. The captain can pass it on to even one man and that man should in turn pass it on so that in the end there are eight or nine who have this same moral fiber, which is nothing more than winning."

In concrete terms, look at the countless times the

Celtics have come down to the final few seconds or even the final game needing a basket to win, and getting it. This comes from the confidence that goes along with character and leadership. Everyone is willing to perform even the most menial task—such as passing the ball just one time—that will enable someone to get the shot that wins the game. Havlicek has made many, many of these game-winning shots but says he doesn't really look upon them as any great accomplishment.

"The man who has the toughest job in a last-ditch situation like that is the man who takes the ball out of bounds," he says. "If he doesn't trigger the play, it goes nowhere. For many years, Don Nelson was that man for us. When he'd get it to me all I would do was shoot it and try my best.

"If you do that, no one can ask any more. If you make a bad pass, then you're wearing the goat horns. That's the type of thing, in my mind, which is tougher than taking the shot."

He has gone through some tough times as captain, too, particularly during the two years following Russell's retirement when the Celtics were being rebuilt into another championship team. Havlicek went from being one of the youngest of the Celtics to one of the oldest, when White, Cowens, and Don Chaney began reshaping the Celtics of the seventies.

"At that point," he recalls, "I felt I more or less had to go along with the likes of Nelson and Tom Sanders to keep carrying on the Celtics tradition. That second year

172

we improved on our record even though we were not a great team and the next year we did better still and made the playoffs. But with so many new people who didn't understand the game and our type of play, the whole process was made a bit more difficult from the standpoint of going from a veteran team that made few mistakes to a young team that had to learn by making mistakes."

Sanders, now Boston's coach who also has been Harvard's head coach, feels that Havlicek's leadership was the correct tonic for the correct time. It was quiet and he went out to show the other players how the game should be played, asking only that they follow his example. He occasionally would take a player aside and very discreetly tell him how he could do better. He had the right touch, so to speak, with a young player trying to make a career with the best basketball team in history.

What makes such situations tough on players like Havlicek who demand excellence of themselves is to remember that a captain is not a coach. Thus, he never can step across the line and take the coach's responsibilities unless asked. He can ease the burden of the coach a bit, as he has been asked to do, but never can he order or demand. Havlicek has said on several occasions that he finds it harder to reconcile the differences in players coming into the sport now than when he joined the Celtics in the early sixties.

"The game hasn't changed, but the players have," he notes. "They are much bigger, faster, and quicker now and have a great physical edge. So there is a tendency to expect more from them. But they are not as good fundamentally as the players who came into the game when I did. They'll take the short cut and try to outjump an opponent instead of blocking out properly."

He won't run a clinic to try and improve them, preferring to deal with the areas he feels most comfortable with on a person-to-person basis, as he did this year with Stacom. He will listen to any problem his teammates will bring to him and if they ask him to talk to the coach, he'll do so. He doesn't try to sort out the problems according to merit but will talk it out with the player. If it must go further, he'll go directly to his coach so as to short-stop any potential trouble area that could hurt the team.

Heinsohn feels that Havlicek's relationship with the players and his preference to lead by example are the best possible combination for helping the Celtics. He points to the reason John was chosen for the job: "He epitomized what a Celtic should be . . . a hustling type of player, a guy who would go into the stands for the ball. When the other players saw a great player like John doing these things, that we put the official sanction on it, they understood that this is what made him a great ballplayer. He became the perfect example and people followed him by example rather than depending on what he said."

Tom also calls Havlicek "the coach's ear with the players." This is necessary because the coach cannot always go to the players, and the captain can do much of his coach's advance work by talking to a player and trying to convince him he should be doing things a certain way. Add the coach's efforts in this same direction and the player soon will get the message. What he does with it depends entirely on him. The fact that the Celtics have had little failures in this area shows how strong the leadership has been . . . from the top, where Auerbach is general manager, to the coach and captain. There is only one method of doing things on the team and strict adherence to that method is demanded. No one in this chain of command ever will undercut the other's authority or attempt to lessen his impact.

There was a time when Heinsohn gave Havlicek almost as much authority over the players as he himself held.

"I was new to coaching and I needed help," Tom recalls. "I went to John and offered him carte blanche powers as my assistant and he accepted. I'll admit it was an unusual thing to do and a lot of guys might have taken advantage of such a situation. But I knew I never would have to worry with Havlicek. So I let him run things for me on the floor and I urged him to go over the mistakes of our young players with them during plane trips or whenever he felt like it.

"It was tough on John during a game because we used him as a forward most of the time whereas most teams allow a guard to run their offense. But he did a tremendous job. Later, we hired an assistant coach to help me on the bench and with scouting, and allowed John to concentrate on working in a game."

Auerbach notes that John's captaincy and his role with the team exceeded anything that Cousy, for example, was given. Havlicek's judgments most often were precise and while he didn't always agree with everything Heinsohn designed he put his own whims aside and worked to make it successful.

John's knowledge of the rules is another area—important for any captain—that has often worked to the Celtics' advantage. When the Celtics played the Philadelphia 76ers at the Spectrum in Philadelphia several years ago, Havlicek noticed that the foul lanes had been repainted and didn't seem to be the required sixteen feet apart. The 76ers had Wilt Chamberlain playing center at the time, so any such advantage clearly would work to their benefit. John asked that the lanes be measured, and sure enough they were only fourteen feet apart.

A couple of years ago, Havlicek's well-trained eye detected that one of the baskets in Chicago Stadium seemed lower than the other—the one the hometown Bulls would use in the second half. Again, he asked for a measurement and again he was correct . . . by two inches. The game was late starting that night until the basket was properly positioned.

There have been countless times when Havlicek has stopped play during out-of-bound situations when he felt the opposition was not lining up according to the rules. In fact, he bet one referee a steak dinner on a rules interpretation and was declared correct.

176

"He still owes me and I have it hanging over his head," Havlicek says with a laugh.

His dealings with officials are an integral part of his duties during a game. There isn't a player in the NBA more respected by the officials and they will stop and listen to his reasoning. They may not agree and that steak dinner shows that sometimes they should. They know too that Havlicek does not chronically complain about foul calls, and when he does there usually is some justification.

How can you tell?

If John raises his hand after he has been charged with a foul, he agrees with the official's call. If he doesn't he won't raise it until ordered to do so, and even then it will be rather half-hearted.

"The thing I'll talk most about to an official, other than a clear misunderstanding of the rules, will be his poor position to make a proper call. Or I'll simply tell him he missed the play. I don't think everyone is perfect, so all I want them to do is to look at the situation from the viewpoint, 'Maybe I did miss one I can talk to all of them and I know I have their respect. That's really all you can ask."

That is basic John Havlicek.

John has a formula to success he will tell anyone who asks:

"Everyone knows the basic difference between right and wrong. If you can put more rights than wrongs on your side of the ledger then you'll be successful. If you can achieve that and lead by example, then you'll end up influencing people by being the type of person who may have an effect and achieve a role as a good captain . . . or, more importantly, as a good person."

And John Havlicek certainly is all of that.